Karin Greiner / Dr. Angelika Weber

House-
plants

from A to Z

➤ The best plants for a beautiful home
➤ Design ideas for every room and location

BARRON'S

Contents

Selecting Plants

The Plant Profiles

Designing with Plants

Appendix

Selecting Plants

To make the right choices from the
enormous range of houseplants,
you need to be well informed about
the kind of location and care each
plant requires. When these needs
are met, your efforts quickly will
be rewarded with lush flowers
and foliage.

Origin and Requirements

Houseplants are living entities that have to thrive in isolation from their native habitats. At the same time, they are completely dependent on the attention you bestow. If you pamper your indoor plants by giving them the conditions they are accustomed to in their native surroundings, they will repay you with lush, abundant growth.

Where Do They Come From?

The history of pot culture dates back thousands of years, and over the course of time the available supply of houseplants has steadily expanded. Exploration and study of plants throughout the world has brought into our living rooms increasing numbers of new species that

Desert plants are used to dryness and heat.

In a tropical rain forest, the atmospheric humidity is high.

originated in totally different climate areas.

Most houseplants are natives of tropical and subtropical regions. This is attributable on the one hand to the extraordinary effect that exotic plants have on us, and on the other to the difficulty of year-round cultivation of domestic species indoors, where they miss winter's cold temperatures. Tropical and subtropical plants, however, are not subject to serious interruptions of growth due to prolonged cold weather; they are accustomed to permanent warmth. Since their very origin tells us much about the plants' needs, you will find "Origin" listed as a separate category in the plant profile section. By using the information on habitat and the rough geographic orientation, you can draw conclusions about the right location and care for your plants.

➤ Plants from tropical rain forests want things warm and damp all year, and they don't tolerate direct sun. These natives of tropical forests kept green by abundant rainfall are used to a warm, humid climate with a cooler and drier winter phase.

➤ Plants from tropical mountain forests like bright, humid conditions, tolerate somewhat cooler temperatures, and usually need a porous substrate and very little fertilizer.

➤ Grasslands and deserts are home to species that enjoy sun and aridity. These plants usually observe a period of dormancy.

➤ Plants that originated in Mediterranean sclerophyllous forests want warm, dry, sunny conditions in summer, but prefer things cool and only slightly humid in winter. During the summer, such species also can be placed outdoors.

The Right Location

If you choose the optimum location for your indoor plants, they will be a constant source of sheer delight. If the lighting, temperature, and humidity are right, then you've already met the basic requirements for exuberant growth.

What Plants Need

➤ **Light:** Every plant needs light to live, some more, some less. Real sun worshippers like desert plants will thrive only if they are always in blazing sunlight. Shade-lovers, such as many ferns that are natives of dark forests, are content with dim light. Keep in mind that the light intensity is far lower indoors than outdoors, and the farther you are from a window, the more it decreases. A spot in the room that you think of as fairly bright may be too dark for plants. Plants require a quality of light that generally is available only near windows. Next to a window, 100 percent of the light intensity reaches the plant, but this figure diminishes with distance: 3 feet (1 m) away, only 50 to 80 percent of the light is available, 5 feet (1.5 m) away, only 25–50 percent, and 6.5 feet (2 m) away, a scant 10–25 percent. In winter, if not sooner, this can become a serious problem for plants.

➤ **Temperature:** Depending on their origin, houseplants prefer certain temperatures. Tropical plants want much warmer positions than Mediterranean natives. While some are tolerant, others may "catch cold" even if the variations in temperature are slight.

Special lamps allow plants to thrive even if placed in the center of the room.

Additional Lighting
Use special energy-providing and fluorescent tubes whose light spectrum is an exact match for the requirements of houseplants. They shed light evenly and are intended for lighting relatively large areas or groups of plants. Spot lamps are suitable for solitary plants, while lamps that distribute light broadly are best for small areas with few plants or for a single large specimen.

The temperature in winter is of primary importance. Consider whether the plants need a warm location year round or prefer to be cooler during their winter rest.

➤ **Air humidity:** This factor too must help determine your choice of location. Plants need an average atmospheric humidity level of 50 to 60 percent; species from tropical rain forests need as much as 80 percent. A very few can get by with dry air. While atmospheric humidity usually is not problematic in summer, in winter it often can fall below 30 percent in heated surroundings: an unhealthy level for plants. To remedy the situation, you can use air humidifiers or indoor

The best place for houseplants usually is right next to the window.

fountains and mist the plants regularly.

On the Windowsill
Certainly windowsills are the locations most often chosen for indoor plants—because they are closest to the light source and also look their loveliest there. The available space on your side of the windowpane should be wide enough to accommodate the chosen plant comfortably. Large windows offer optimal light conditions, as do skylight windows or dormer windows with glass on all sides. Curtains or shades swallow a great deal of light, even if they are transparent. Nearby buildings, trees, and the like can also take away much of the light. Radiators under the windows will result in dry air in winter. ➤ **South-facing windows** naturally offer the most light, but they also admit

A gorgeous specimen like this deserves a special location.

blazing sunlight, at least at midday. In addition, the air behind the pane heats up quickly. This is the right location for sun-loving and drought-tolerant plants like cacti and other succulents.

➤ **East- and west-facing windows** offer morning or evening sun, but during the day they admit plenty of light without burning rays. These windows are ideal for plants that need a bright location, but do not tolerate the blazing sun.

➤ **North-facing windows** do not receive the direct sun. Shade-tolerant plants grow best in the mild daylight available here.

Out in the Room

Large, spreading plants in particular are unlikely to have enough room on windowsills and should be placed elsewhere in the room. The best conditions for them are offered by rooms with glassed-in sides, balcony doors, or patio doors, behind which the plants can be set directly on the floor or on suitable pieces of furniture. Closer to the center of the room, it is advisable to check to see

---

EXTRA TIP

Displaying Houseplants

Columns and pedestals are ideal for putting the focus on decorative solo plants like the ficus or for showing hanging plants to their best advantage. Benches at various heights offer room for several plants in a grouping. Etageres will make plants easy to see on several levels at once. Low stools and platforms are well suited for plants that are more effective if placed slightly above floor level, such as strawberry begonia.

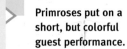

Primroses put on a short, but colorful guest performance.

whether an additional light source is necessary. For large, heavy plants, a stand on wheels is a good idea, so that you can push them back and forth with no trouble.

Companions Wanted

Do you want a plant to keep you company with its green foliage for a period of years, perhaps delighting you with an annual display of blossoms? Then you need to use perennials, ideally trees and shrubs such as rubber trees or azaleas (→ short summaries in the plant profiles). Sago palms, orchids, or tuberous plants such as cyclamen are considered quite long-lived companions—provided they have the right location and attentive care.

Although you can't expect short-lived plants to give you long-term friendship, they often will provide an abundance of flowers and opulent foliage. Moreover, plants that complete their life cycle in only a few months generally need no intensive care, but they do offer great, though brief, pleasure. Their advantage: You can quickly add new accents, bring a splash of color into your home, and keep redecorating without major expenditures. In addition to the true annuals, very short-lived species such as painted nettle (coleus) and impatiens offer their benefits only briefly, since they quickly fade and lose their looks. Similarly, seasonal plants such as primrose or hyacinth last only a few weeks indoors. The term "throwaway plants" is used for species like kalanchoe that are difficult to maintain after they finish flowering. African violets, azaleas, and poinsettias also are discarded in this way, although they actually are long-lived.

Where to Buy

The biggest selection of indoor plants is available in nurseries and garden centers. You can rely on their generally high quality and good advice when you want to buy long-lived, high-priced plants. Short-lived and seasonal plants can easily be acquired at a supermarket as well.

Always look for plants that seem healthy and vibrant, "full of sap," so to speak. Yellowed, spotted, rotting leaves, shoots that have

> **Long-lived large plants are best purchased from nurseries or plant shops.**

snapped off, withered buds, soft spots on bulbs or tubers, algae or moss deposits on the substrate, or roots that are growing out of the pot are always signs of unprofessional care, pest infestation, or deficiencies. Leave such specimens on the shelf.

Well Potted

Matching the right pot with the right plant can make all

the difference—and you need to keep this in mind when choosing planters. Houseplants are necessarily potted plants; their roots can develop only in a container full of a growing medium, or substrate.

➤ **The Size:** A plant is in the right pot when it is neither too small nor too large. The root system must have room to develop sufficiently, but not too much room. The size of the pot should harmonize with the overall plant.

➤ **The Material:** Whether you raise plants in a clay pot or a plastic one is a matter of personal taste. Both have their advantages. The porous clay pots provide better aeration for the roots, and the substrate dries more quickly. However, the soil also dries out more quickly.

Indoor hydroponic culture is an especially easy way to grow plants.

If you enjoy watering and are inclined to water a bit too much on occasion, clay pots are the right choice for you. In plastic pots the roots develop much more uniformly and moisture is retained longer, but waterlogging can develop quickly. If you are inclined to water sparingly, these pots are highly recommended. Special plants demand special planters: Palms with long, deep roots should be put in tall palm pots. For plants with shallow roots, such as cacti, bowls make adequate containers.

The root systems of orchids, as well as bromeliads, require especially good aeration, and they do best in special orchid pots with pierced sides or latticework

➤ **The Substrate:** Generally, houseplants find everything they need in commercially available potting soil. The substrate must be loose, air-permeable, and stable in structure, and it must be able to absorb water immediately and retain it. It also has to store nutrients successfully and have the correct pH. The following earmarks will tell you whether a plant is potted

Shallow-rooted plants also grow well in low, shallow planters.

in high-quality soil: It is securely held by the surrounding medium and cannot be pulled out with a slight tug. The substrate is fine and crumbly and feels slightly damp. It is not clumpy, and there are no signs of coatings or any mold. The soil has a pleasant woodsy smell. If these features are not present, you should repot the plant without delay. Some houseplants also grow readily in hydroponic culture (→ page 17).

Technical Terms from A to Z

➤ Air-layering
Method of propagation by which roots are stimulated to grow from a part of the stem, cut halfway through and wrapped in a moist material. The newly rooted part can be cut off and potted in its own container. In principle, similar to taking a → cutting.

➤ Annuals
Plants that live for only one year or season.

➤ Clay granules
Special → substrate consisting of fine-grained pieces of clay, which can store water. Usually used in place of soil mixtures. A humidity sensor indicates when it is time to add water again.

➤ Cultivar
Special cultivated variety of a → species that has disting-uishable features, such as a special flower color or growth habit. A cultivar name is indicated by a word in single quotation marks following the species name, such as *Acalypha hispida* 'Alba.'

➤ Cutting back
Moderately trimming parts of stems, especially branches of → trees and → shrubs. The cut should always be made with sharp shears at an angle, just above a leaf bud. Cutting back hard involves shortening the stems to just a few centimeters. Generally, however, cut back by one-third.

➤ Cuttings
Plant parts, especially from stem tips (tip cuttings), mature sprouts (stem cuttings), or leaves (leaf cuttings), that are cut off plants for propagation and stuck in substrate to take root. For plants that strike root readily, place cuttings in a glass of water and pot them after the roots have formed.

➤ Dark germinators
Plants whose seeds require complete darkness to germinate. The seed must be carefully covered at all times. See also → light germinators.

➤ Division
Method of propagation in which a well-developed plant is simply separated into two or more parts. Each part must have healthy roots and at least one vigorous stem or stem tip.

➤ Drainage
In container culture, a bottom layer of coarse gravel, pebbles, or pieces of bricks is placed in the container. It allows excess water to run off quickly, thus preventing → waterlogging.

➤ **Epiphytes**
Plants that naturally grow in the crowns or branches of trees, such as many orchids and bromeliads. They often develop aerial roots, which they use to absorb water and nutrients from the surrounding air.

➤ **Expanded clay**
Pellets made of fired clay in various sizes, used as a growing medium in → hydroponic culture. Unlike → clay granules, expanded clay does not hold water.

➤ **Family**
In botany, the term for a group of related plants; its scientific name ends in → *aceae*, as in *Begoniaceae*. It is the classification level above genus.

➤ **Fertilizing / Feeding**
Adding nutrients to plants. Fertilizer can be provided in solid form (for example, as spikes or cones) or in liquid form (added to the watering can). Complete fertilizers supply plants with all the important nutrients. Special fertilizers are tailored to the specific needs of plants such as cacti, azaleas, and orchids. Follow the manufacturer's recommended dosages. From September to March, do not feed your plants, with the exception of flowering species.

➤ **Flower window**
Large window suitable for growing houseplants, with a broad windowsill. The side facing the room may also be glassed in to create a kind of hothouse. See also → mini-greenhouse.

➤ **Genus**
Term for a group of → species that are closely related and have common characteristics.

➤ **Herbaceous perennial**
Form of perennial that has soft, nonwoody stems. Its growth habit is quite variable, ranging from stiffly upright to creeping or hanging.

➤ **Hybrid**
Cross of two or more → species, which combines characteristics of both parents. In botanical nomenclature, its name contains an x between the genus name and the species name: *Begonia* x *ricinifolia*. A group of hybrids with a defined origin or special properties often is given a name of its own, such as *Anthurium scherzerianum* hybrids. Intergeneric (bigeneric) hybrids result from a

17

crossing of plants that belong to different genera (→ genus); their names contain an x before the botanical name: x *Fatshedera lizei*.

➤ **Hydroponic culture (hydroponics, hydroculture)**
Type of culture in which plants are grown in special double containers without soil, in expanded clay and a nutrient solution of water and a fertilizer additive. A water gauge indicates the water level in the container. The plant absorbs exactly as much water as it needs. Thus the risk of watering or feeding the plant improperly is quite low.

➤ **Immersion**
A method of watering, in which the entire container is immersed in water that reaches just over the rim of the pot until no more air bubbles appear and the soil is saturated. In conclusion, carefully let excess water drip out.

➤ **Light germinators**
Plants whose seeds germinate only under the influence of light. The seed should be left uncovered or given only a light sprinkling of soil. See also → dark germinators.

➤ **Mini-greenhouse**
Small indoor hothouse, often resembling a glassed-in → flower window or garden window, equipped with a heater, a misting system, ventilation, and additional lighting.

➤ **Misting**
Care procedure intended to moisturize dry air. Plants are misted with a spray bottle containing lime-free water at room temperature.

➤ **Offsets**
Young plants that in some species develop right next to the parent plant. They can be used for propagation.

➤ **Pinch out (pinch back)**
Pinching with the fingers or cutting off the tips of shoots or buds to promote branching and encourage compact growth.

➤ **Plantlets**
Young plants that develop on the leaves or stems of some plants and can be removed for propagation and potted.

➤ **Pseudobulbs**
Thickened, bulblike stems of orchids that arise from a vertical part of a main stem.

➤ **Seasonal plant**
Plant that is sold at a certain time of year and is grown indoors for only a short time.

➤ **Shrub**
A perennial woody plant, having several stems arising from the base rather than a single trunk, in contrast to a → tree.

➤ **Species**
In botany, a category of classification for plants with common attributes. A plant species has a two-part scientific name, such as *Aspidistra elatior*. The first indicates the genus; the second is the specific epithet.

➤ **Subshrub**
Perennial plant with multiple woody stems at the base and growth at the top that remains herbaceous, in contrast to a → shrub.

➤ **Substrate**
Predominantly industrially produced soil, usually made of various components such as peat and clay, or of different components such as → clay granules or → expanded clay, as in → hydroponic culture.

➤ **Succulent**
Plant that can store water in its leaves, stems, or other organs. Cacti and many euphorbias and agaves are succulents.

➤ **Tree**
A perennial woody plant that forms a main trunk bearing a branching crown, in contrast to a → shrub.

➤ **Variegation**
Variability in leaf coloration and marking, as in the form of striation or mottling, of natural origin or deliberately cultivated.

➤ **Waterlogging**
State in which the soil is constantly saturated with water, so that excess moisture cannot run off at all or in sufficient amounts. It can lead to root rot and decay and can be prevented by good → drainage.

The Plant Profiles

Here you'll find tips on care and summaries of important information about the 200 most popular houseplants. They are divided into three large groups: flowering plants, foliage plants, and cacti and other succulents.

Structure of the Profiles

The houseplants on the following pages are divided into three large groups: flowering plants, including orchids and some bromeliads as well; foliage plants, along with palms, ferns, grasses, and bromeliads that lack showy flowers; and cacti and other succulents.

The Plant Profiles

All the profiles are divided into categories. Sometimes a few of the categories are omitted if they are irrelevant for the plant in question. For example, in the section containing foliage plants, there is no information on flowers.

The profiles are alphabetized according to the plants' botanical names, which appear in italics at the head of the entry. If only one species is described here, you will find the species name in that location. It always has two parts: the genus name—*Hoya*, for example—appears first, and the species name—*bella*, for example—follows. Thus the wax plant is *Hoya bella*. If several species are discussed, the term "species" is added to the genus name, and if there are several cultivars, the term "hybrids" is added.

Next, in boldface and larger type, is the most frequently used common name of the plant. In addition to the photos, the symbol bar (→ next page) will help orient you quickly, as will the categories describing the characteristic growth form, or habit, of the plant and its flowering period, if any.

Under the following headings, you will find everything you need to know about the plants:

Other names: Additional common names, or information about possible name changes

Family: Common name and botanical (scientific) name

Origin: Original habitat and geographical range

Flowers: Description of color, shape, time of flowering, and fruit

Appearance: Growth habit and characteristics, as well as color, shape, and properties of the leaves

Location: Information about light and temperature requirements, including needs during overwintering

Care: Information about watering, fertilizing, misting, and, if applicable, trimming and methods and times for propagation
Use: Suitability for certain locations or design suggestions
Note: Information about toxicity, possibility of skin irritation, or other noteworthy features
Cultivars/Relatives: Other cultivars or species not described in the main text

 Suitable for beginners, as it is very low-maintenance (follow guidelines for location requirements and advice on care).

 The plant prefers a predominantly sunny location.

 The plant likes a bright location, but not in the blazing sun.

 The plant does best in partial shade.

 The plant will thrive even in shade.

 Water generously (roughly every two to three days).

 Water moderately (about once a week).

 Water sparingly (plant can tolerate short periods of dryness).

 The plant likes high atmospheric humidity; mist frequently.

 Decorative in hanging planters and baskets.

 The plant must be trained to climb with the right kind of support.

 Suitable for hydroponic culture.

 Seasonal plant; often cultivated only during the bloom.

 Intense scent produced by flowers and/or leaves.

 The plant contains toxins or skin irritants.

Flowering Plants
from A to Z

An intoxicating abundance of blossoms or single graceful blooms, blazingly bright colors or tender pastel hues—flowering plants are rightly considered the superstars of houseplants. Because their fruit can be equally striking, the following profiles also include plants that produce lovely, eye-catching, and long-lasting fruit.

Growth form:
Shrub
Flowering period:
Feb.–Oct.

Acalypha hispida
Chenille Plant

Family: Spurge (*Euphorbiaceae*)
Origin: Worldwide in tropics and subtropics
Flowers: Red inflorescences resembling bottle brushes that hang down, up to 19 inches (50 cm) long; February–October
Appearance: Bushy, compact growth; large, dark green leaves with serrate margins
Location: Bright, but not in full sun, warm and protected all year round, even in winter not below 60°F (16°C)
Care: During the flowering period, keep evenly damp and fertilize every two weeks, less often in winter; mist often with lukewarm soft water to prevent pest infestation; propagate from tip cuttings in spring, with soil temperature of at least 68°F (20°C) and high air humidity
Use: Pretty flowering plant for bright windows
Note: All parts of the plant are toxic.
Cultivars/Relatives: 'Alba' has white flowers; *A. hispaniolae* is daintier and even more pendulous.

Growth form:
Herbaceous perennial
Flowering period:
July–Sept.

Achimenes Hybrids

Magic Flowers

Family: Gesneriad (*Gesneriaceae*)
Origin: Tropics of Central and South America
Flowers: Plate-shaped, asymmetrical; white, yellow, pink, violet, blue; July–September
Appearance: Bush-forming, produces scaly, cone-shaped rhizomes; leaves are ovate, pointed, light green, partly reddish underneath
Location: In summer, bright and warm, never in full sun
Care: Keep evenly damp in the flowering period, no cold water; until early August feed every two weeks; gradually discontinue watering; to overwinter, let rhizomes die back and store them dry in sphagnum at 50°F (10°C), then from January place them in fresh soil to incite growth; propagate from tip cuttings or by rhizome division
Use: Seasonal decoration for bright windows; pendant cultivars well suited for hanging planters
Cultivars/Relatives: Hybrids are almost the only such plants commercially available; generally cultivars are not named.

Growth form: *Herbaceous perennial*
Flowering period: *May–Oct.*

Aechmea fasciata

Silver Vase ✿

Family: Bromeliads (*Bromeliaceae*)
Origin: Tropical and subtropical Central and South America
Flowers: Panicled or fascicular inflorescence with pink bracts; May-October
Appearance: Grows as funnel-shaped rosette, in which the inflorescence develops; leaves are broadly lanceolate, stiff, with toothed margins, easily up to 19 inches (50 cm) long, usually banded and "frosted"
Location: Bright, without direct sun; warm, even in winter above 64°F (18°C)
Care: From spring to fall, always keep evenly damp with lime-free water; over the summer keep water in the rosette as well, but without fertilizer; in winter water with restraint; feed every two weeks; regularly remove faded, withering rosettes
Use: Very low-maintenance flowering and ornamental foliage plant for bright rooms and flower windows
Note: The plant sap may cause skin irritations.

Growth form: *Subshrub*
Flowering period: *June–Sept.*

Aeschynanthus radicans

Lipstick Plant

Other names: Basketvine
Family: Gesneriad (*Gesneriaceae*)
Origin: Tropical rain forests of Southeast Asia
Flowers: Red to orange terminal clusters, paired at the stem tips; June–September
Appearance: Full, bushy subshrub, upright at first, later pendant; evergreen, leathery leaves
Location: Bright, but not in blazing sun; very warm and humid air, in winter also moderately warm at 64°F (18°C)
Care: Keep moderately damp, drier in winter (use lime-free water); until August fertilize every two weeks; mist frequently; propagation from tip cuttings
Use: For hanging planters in flower windows, warm conservatories, also for bright living room windows
Note: Flowers drop if the dampness of the substrate fluctuates and the temperature varies.
Cultivars/Relatives: *A.* x *splendidus* with brownish mottling, *A. speciosus* with slimmer tubular flowers.

Growth form:
Climbing shrub
Flowering period:
May–Nov.

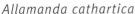

Allamanda cathartica

Allamanda

Other names: Golden trumpet vine, yellow bell
Family: Dogbane (*Apocynaceae*)
Origin: Tropical South America
Flowers: Yellow bells; scented; May–November
Appearance: Energetic twining vine with ovate, dark green leaves, evergreen
Location: Very bright, also in full sun and humid air; warm all year round at 64–77°F (18–25°C)
Care: Keep evenly damp, water more sparingly in winter; mist frequently; feed weekly until August; provide stable climbing aid; cut back hard in February to promote flower production and branching; propagate from tip or stem cuttings
Use: Marvelous ornamental flowers for large, bright windows and for warm conservatories
Note: The plant can climb to a height of 13 feet (4 m); all parts are poisonous.
Cultivars/Relatives: 'Grandiflora,' yellow flowers; 'Hendersonii,' orange-yellow flowers; *A. blanchetii*, violet flowers.

Growth form: *Herbaceous perennial*
Flowering period: *Depends on cultivation*

Ananas comosus

Pineapple

Family: Bromeliad (*Bromeliaceae*)
Origin: Tropical Central and South America
Flowers: Conical inflorescence with reddish bracts, above which tuftlike leaves appear in older plants, under ideal conditions
Appearance: Spreading growth, loose rosette of leaves from which the inflorescence emerges; narrow leaves with thickened, spiny margins and white to yellowish stripes near the margins
Location: Preferably bright, no blazing sun; warm all year round; good aeration
Care: During growth period, keep well dampened with lime-poor water and fertilize weekly in moderation; reduce watering and feeding in winter; propagate from offsets
Use: Flowering and foliage plant that needs plenty of space; also suitable as a solitary specimen
Cultivars/Relatives: *A. bracteatus* has yellow leaf margins and red bracts; the leaf margins of *A. comosus* 'Variegatus' (→ photo) are white.

Growth form:
Herbaceous perennial
Flowering period:
May–June

Anigozanthos Hybrids
Kangaroo Paw

Family: Bloodwort (*Haemodoraceae*)
Origin: Arid regions of Australia
Flowers: Long-stemmed; yellowish, green, or pink; short flower spikes resemble a hairy kangaroo paw; May–June
Appearance: Grows upright as a bushy herbaceous perennial, produces large rhizomes; long, narrow, lanceolate leaves
Location: Water amply in summer and fertilize in moderation every two weeks, but only with decalcified water and lime-free fertilizer, such as azalea food; as substrate use acid soil, mixed with some sand; older plants can be divided carefully
Use: Graceful ornamental flower; tall cultivars and species can be grown in container, low ones on the windowsill; pretty, attractive summer decoration for balcony or patio

Growth form: *Herbaceous perennial*
Flowering period: *Spring–fall, also all year round*

Anthurium Hybrids

Flamingo Flower

Other names: Anthurium, tailflower
Family: Arum lily (*Araceae*)
Origin: Tropical rain forests of Central and South America
Flowers: Brilliantly colored spathe in red, white, or pink, also spotted, surrounds a long, slender spadix
Appearance: Grows upright, develops short, thicker stems over time, spadix and leaves on long stems; leaves, depending on species, are lanceolate or cordate-ovate, usually dark green and shiny
Location: Bright to part shade and warm, no direct sun; the plants don't like "cold feet"
Care: Keep evenly damp and mist fairly often, avoid waterlogging, water less in winter; use only soft, decalcified water; fertilize every two weeks in growth period, only every four weeks in winter
Use: Pretty on a window ledge or in a flower window
Note: Contact with skin can cause irritation to skin, eyes, and mouth.

Growth form:
Shrub
Flowering period:
April–Oct.

Aphelandra squarrosa

Zebra Plant

Family: Acanthus (*Acanthaceae*)
Origin: Tropical and subtropical forests of Central and South America
Flowers: Yellow bracts that overlap like shingles on a roof, borne in 11½ inch (20-cm) long spikes in which yellow tubular flowers grow; April–October
Appearance: Grows bushy and compact; leaves up to 11½ inch (30 cm) long, with pointed tips, glossy dark green, with striking white leaf veins
Location: Bright and warm, in winter not below 59°F (15°C)
Care: Keep evenly damp, also in winter, and mist often, using only decalcified water at room temperature; fertilize every two weeks; cut back hard in spring
Use: Attractive flowering plant for the windowsill
Cultivars/Relatives: Harder to please are *A. tetragona,* with red bracts and flowers, up to 5 feet (1.5 m) tall, and *A. sinclairiana,* with brick-red bracts and pink flowers.

Growth form:
Herbaceous perennial
Flowering period:
All year round

Begonia elatior Hybrids

Begonia Elatior Hybrids

Family: Begonia (*Begoniaceae*)
Origin: Original species from the tropics of South America
Flowers: Great variety of colors and shapes: single, double, rounded or star-shaped; now commercially available all year
Appearance: Growth is bushy, some cultivars slightly pendent; leaves are asymmetrical, divided by the central rib into two unequal parts
Location: Bright and warm, no direct sun, even in winter not below 64°F (18°C)
Care: Keep evenly and slightly damp; fertilize every two weeks; remove faded flowers and dead plant parts immediately to prevent fungal decay; plants are usually discarded after the bloom, as further cultivation is not really worthwhile
Use: Dependable long-term bloomer for rooms and conservatories, pendant cultivars also in hanging planters
Note: Some are poisonous, with skin irritants.

Growth form: *Herbaceous perennial*
Flowering period: *Predominantly in winter*

Billbergia nutans

Queen's Tears ✿

Family: Bromeliads (*Bromeliaceae*)
Origin: Tropical Central and South America
Flowers: Flower spikes with reddish, overhanging bracts; time of bloom depends on culture, primarily in winter
Appearance: Grows as leaf rosettes, from which the flower shafts protrude; crowding quickly results, due to offset formation; leaves grasslike, up to about 11½ inches (30 cm) long, arching and spilling over
Location: Bright to partial shade, no blazing midday sun; warm and humid air; during summer also outdoors; in winter not below 54°F (12°C)
Care: In summer, keep moderately damp with low-lime water and fertilize weekly; in winter, water sparingly, in a cool location, but don't let the root ball dry out completely; always keep air humidity high by frequent misting with low-lime water
Use: Undemanding houseplant for warm and not overly dark places

Growth form: *Subshrub*
Flowering period: *All year round*

Browallia speciosa

Bush Violet

Other names: Amethyst flower
Family: Nightshade (*Solanaceae*)
Origin: Tropics of South America, principally Colombia
Flowers: Blue, violet, or white single flowers with light throat; all year round in large numbers in the leaf axils
Appearance: Grows as subshrub, up to 19 inches (50 cm) tall; leaves are lanceolate, dark green
Location: Bright to sunny and warm, even in winter do not let temperature drop below 59°F (15°C); at midday in summer, provide with shade next to south-facing windows
Care: From spring to fall, water generously, in winter, somewhat less; in summer, fertilize every two weeks; propagate from seed in spring (light germinator) at 68–77°F (20–25°C) or from cuttings in summer
Use: Pretty and persistent bloomer for sunny rooms
Note: Special growth retardants can produce a compact form; once they have dissipated, the plant gets leggy. Some newer cultivars remain densely bushy.

Growth form:
Shrub
Flowering period:
Feb.–June

Brunfelsia pauciflora var. *calycina*

Yesterday, Today, and Tomorrow

Other names: Morning, noon, and night
Origin: Tropics in South America, chiefly Brazil
Flowers: Large, disc-shaped, violet, strongly scented flowers; in the cultivar 'Eximia,' the color varies over time from violet to pale lilac to white; February–June
Appearance: Grows as evergreen shrub, somewhat leggy; even frequent cutting back and pinching out do not make it much bushier; leathery, elongated, dark green leaves
Location: Bright and warm all year, in winter at 50–57°F (10–14°C) for about eight weeks to stimulate flowering
Care: From spring to fall, keep slightly damp and fertilize every two weeks; in winter, water less and discontinue feeding; mist often; use only low-lime, room-temperature water; requires low-lime substrate; propagate from tip cuttings in sufficiently warm soil (about 77°F [25°C])
Use: Flowering plant for indoor use, also well suited for conservatories
Note: The plant is poisonous, especially the roots.

Growth form: *Herbaceous perennial*
Flowering period: *Jan.–Feb.*

Calathea crocata

Eternal Flame

Family: Prayer-plant (*Marantaceae*)
Origin: Tropical rain forests of Brazil
Flowers: Tall spikes of saffron-yellow, long-lasting, flamelike inflorescences; January–February
Appearance: Clump-forming; leaves and flowers grow on separate long stems; leaves are elongated and oval, dark green on top with maroon undersides
Location: All year round, bright to partially shady, with warm, humid air; cooler in fall and winter, at 64°F (18°C); avoid cold soil temperature and drafts
Care: In spring and summer, water generously with soft water; fertilize every two weeks; starting in fall, reduce watering and feeding, provide no more than ten hours of light daily if you want to induce flowering (short-day treatment); mist frequently; needs loose, coarse soil; propagate by division
Use: Ornamental flowering and foliage plant, best in a warm conservatory or a closed mini-greenhouse

Growth form:
Annual
Flowering period:
Sept.–May

Calceolaria Hybrids

Slipper Flower

Family: Figwort (*Scrophulariaceae*)

Origin: Mountainous regions of South America

Flowers: Slipper-shaped and puffy, yellow, orange, or red, also multicolored, usually with red-brown dots or striping; September–May

Appearance: Grows densely bushy, compact, short-lived; leaves are oval, soft, and downy

Location: Bright, but not in full sun, which can easily burn the leaves; cool, at 59–64°F (15–18°C); in winter, below 46°F (8°C) for at least three weeks, otherwise plant will not flower

Care: Water amply to keep root ball always damp, but avoid waterlogging; fertilize weekly; propagate from seed by sowing the minuscule seeds in summer (difficult)

Use: Lush display of brightly colored flowers for cool rooms and bright windowsills with no radiator underneath, also suitable for balconies and patios

Note: The flowering period usually is six to eight weeks, and then the plants are discarded; further cultivation is not really worthwhile.

Growth form:
Shrub
Flowering period:
Fall–spring

Camellia Hybrids

Camellia

Family: Tea (*Theaceae*)
Origin: Humid mountain forests of East Asia
Flowers: Pink, red, white; single, semidouble, or double; in early spring or starting in fall
Appearance: Grows as evergreen shrub, in container culture up to 6.5 feet (2 m) tall; leaves broad and ovate, dark green
Location: Bright or in part shade, no blazing sun, rather cool (not over 64°F [18°C]) and with humid air, in summer also outdoors, in fall and winter at 41–46°F (5–8°C) until flowers open, airy spot but without drafts, during flowering period at 59–64°F (15–18°C), can be in somewhat warmer place when in full bloom
Care: Keep moderately damp and mist regularly, use only low-lime water; in summer, provide with azalea food every two weeks
Use: Winter and spring bloomer for conservatories; there are special cultivars for indoor culture
Note: To prevent bud or flower drop, avoid changing locations.

Growth form:
Herbaceous perennial
Flowering period:
Summer

Campanula Species

Bellflower

Family: Bellflower (*Campanulaceae*)
Origin: Rocky regions of Central and Southern Europe
Flowers: Blue, violet-blue, or white; in the Italian bellflower, (*C. isophylla* → photo) open and star-shaped, June–September; *C. fragilis* has many smaller bell-shaped flowers, May–July
Appearance: Grows prostrate to hanging; all parts of *C. fragilis* stay more delicate; leaves small and stalked, heart-shaped, fresh green color
Location: Bright, also sunny or with part shade; not overly warm, airy, in summer also outdoors; throughout winter cool, at 41°F (5°C), not over 59°F (15°C)
Care: In summer, keep damp and fertilize weekly; cut back long stems after flower production; then keep quite dry until spring; propagate in peat-sand mixture from tip cuttings or by division in spring; *C. isophylla* also from seed (light germinator)
Use: Pretty bloomers for cool, not overly dark rooms; *C. fragilis* usually is grown only as an annual

Growth form: *Herbaceous perennial*
Flowering period: *Summer*

Capsicum annuum

Ornamental Pepper

Other names: Christmas pepper
Family: Nightshade (*Solanaceae*)
Origin: Tropical Central and South America
Flowers: Small, inconspicuous, appearing in early summer; as fall approaches they develop into numerous fruits, depending on cultivar, yellow, orange, red, or violet, ovate or conical; fruit edible but usually quite spicy
Appearance: Bushy, branching growth, up to 15 inches (40 cm) tall; leaves lanceolate, vibrant green
Location: Bright, also sunny; quite cool, not over 68°F (20°C); from late fall at only 59°F (15°C) (fruit lasts longer)
Care: Keep evenly damp, don't overwater; fertilize weekly; propagate from seed in spring at high germination temperatures
Use: Ornamental fruit-bearing plant for bright, cool rooms; usually sold as a seasonal decorative plant for fall and discarded after the fruit dries up in winter
Note: The plant leaves and stems are poisonous, but the fruit is not.

Growth form:
Shrub
Flowering period:
March–Oct.

Catharanthus roseus

Madagascar Periwinkle

Family: Dogbane (*Apocynaceae*)
Origin: Tropical regions of Madagascar and India
Flowers: Plate-shaped; white, pink, or red with darker eye;
March–October
Appearance: Grows shrubby, sprawling; leaves are elongated,
lanceolate, shiny dark green with lighter midrib
Location: Bright, but not blazing midday sun; warm and
humid air; in summer also outdoors, in a spot protected
from rain; overwintering at no less than 54°F (12°C)
Care: In summer keep well dampened but not too wet, mist
frequently; fertilize every two weeks; during overwintering
do not let root ball dry out, in spring cut back and repot;
propagate from tip cuttings in August or from seed in spring
Use: Flowering plant for bright, warm rooms; usually grown
for only one year, since it often is less attractive and has fewer
blooms in the second year
Note: The entire plant is considered extremely poisonous.

Growth form: *Herbaceous perennial*
Flowering period: *Depends on species and cultivar*

Cattleya Species and Hybrids

Cattleya Orchid

Family: Orchid (*Orchidaceae*)
Origin: Tropical Central and South America
Flowers: Large, with tube-shaped lip in racemose inflorescence; white, yellow, shades of pink, red, or violet
Appearance: Epiphytic in its native habitat; cylindrical pseudobulbs; one or two to three leaves on each, depending on form group; leaves elongated and oval, leathery, fleshy
Location: Very bright, not sunny; humid air and well ventilated; keep at 64–75°F (18–24°C), in winter cooler (60°F [16°C]) for two or three months
Care: Water copiously in summer using soft water, let substrate dry between waterings; in winter, water just enough to keep pseudobulbs from withering; mist leaves often; fertilize sparingly each month in growth period
Use: As a solitary specimen in a flower window; robust plants also in rooms
Cultivars/Relatives: *C. bowringiana* (→ photo) is less sensitive; the cultivars of the intergenus hybrid x *Laeliocattleya* also are considered more robust.

Growth form:
Herbaceous perennial
Flowering period:
June–Aug.

Chrysothemis Species

Chrysothemis

Family: Gesneriad (*Gesneriaceae*)
Origin: Tropical Central and South America
Flowers: In *C. pulchella* (→ photo), brilliant yellow with orange-red throat; in *C. friedrichsthaliana*, orange-yellow with yellow or green throat; blooms in summer
Appearance: Grows erect, bushy; herbaceous perennials gradually die back in fall; leaves rough, large, glossy dark green, with striking, notched veining
Location: Bright, but not in direct sun; warm all year round, even in winter not below 59°F (15°C)
Care: Starting in spring, keep moderately damp; fertilize weekly or every two weeks; in fall, gradually water less and keep almost dry after the above-ground parts die back; slowly resume watering after new growth starts in spring; propagate by removing bulblets from leaf axils, from cuttings, or from offsets
Use: Highly decorative flowering and foliage plant for bright, warm rooms

45

Growth form:
Climbing shrub
Flowering period:
April–Sept.

Clerodendrum thomsoniae

Bleeding Heart Vine

Other names: Glory bower, bag flower
Family: Verbena (*Verbenaceae*)
Origin: Tropical regions of West Africa and Cameroon
Flowers: Scarlet red, star-shaped, surrounded by white sepals puffed up like balloons; April–September
Appearance: Vigorous climbing shrub that is kept compact with growth retardants; leaves are large, ovate, dark green
Location: Bright, no blazing sun; warm, humid air; fertilize every one to two weeks until fall; mist fairly often; in winter, water sparingly if in cool place; in spring, cut back and repot; propagate from tip cuttings with plenty of warmth; pinch out young plants fairly often
Use: For bright, warm rooms and conservatories, without growth retardants can be used as climbing plant on a trellis

Growth form:
Herbaceous perennial
Flowering period:
Feb.–May

Clivia miniata

Kaffir Lily

Other names: Bush lily
Family: Amaryllis (*Amaryllidaceae*)
Origin: Dry regions of South Africa
Flowers: Umbel with up to 20 orange or red funnel-shaped flowers on a long stalk; February–May
Appearance: Stem grows out of fleshy leaf sheaths that overlap like onions, from which the arching, overhanging leaves emerge; leaves long, sword-shaped, dark green, glossy
Location: Keep well dampened in summer, no waterlogging; feed every two weeks; cut off inflorescences after bloom, later remove the dying shafts; from September on, gradually water less and stop fertilizing; during dormancy keep cool and almost dry until January; wipe leaves clean occasionally; propagate from lateral scions with at least four leaves
Use: Attractive flowering plant for bright rooms
Note: All parts of the plant are poisonous.

Growth form: *Herbaceous perennial*
Flowering period: *Winter–spring*

Coelogyne Species

Coelogyne

Family: Orchid (*Orchidaceae*)
Origin: Mountain forests of the Himalayas and in East Asia
Flowers: *C. cristata*, white with golden yellow comb on the lip; *C. massangeana*, cream-colored with brown marking, very numerous on a panicle; *C. brachyptera* (→ photo), greenish; other, more rarely available species usually have a whitish ground color; blooms winter to spring
Appearance: Epiphyte; *C. cristata* has roundish pseudobulbs with two leaves each; *C. massangeana* has oblong, one-leaved pseudobulbs; leaves are lanceolate and furrowed
Location: Partial shade; humid, but airy; in summer at room temperature, cooler at night if possible; during winter, *C. cristata* at 53–59°F (12–15°C), *C. massangeana* at 59–68°F (15–20°C)
Care: Keep slightly damp, using soft water; mist fairly often; feed every two to three weeks; keep *C. cristata* almost dry during winter, stop fertilizing; propagate by division
Use: Well suited for east-facing or north-facing windows, especially lovely in hanging planters or orchid baskets

Growth form:
Subshrub
Flowering period:
Spring–late summer

Crossandra infundibuliformis

Firecracker Plant

Other names: Firecracker flower
Family: Acanthus (*Acanthaceae*)
Origin: Tropical forests of Asia
Flowers: Orange-red, salmon pink, or yellow, in spikes that bloom from bottom to top, flowers from spring to late summer
Appearance: Subshrub, grows up to 15 inches (40 cm) tall; leaves are narrow and ovate, slightly wavy, glossy dark green
Location: In summer, in part shade; in winter, bright, warm, and humid, not below 64°F (18°C)
Care: Keep evenly damp with room-temperature, low-lime water and frequently mist leaves (not flowers); from February to August, fertilize weekly; cut back hard after bloom; in winter, keep slightly drier; propagate from tip cuttings in early summer
Use: Decorative flowering and foliage plant for warm rooms, if at all possible with humid air
Note: If the effect of the growth retardants diminishes, the plant must be trimmed frequently.

Growth form: *Herbaceous perennial*
Flowering period: *Summer*

Curcuma zedoaria

Zedoary Root

Other names: White turmeric; frequently also *C. alismatifolia*
Family: Ginger (*Zingiberaceae*)
Origin: Thailand and other Southeast Asia countries
Flowers: In summer, pale pink, bright pink, or white bracts arranged like roof tiles and enclosing the true, inconspicuous, white flowers
Appearance: Herbaceous perennial with tuberous rhizome, from which stiffly erect leaves and sturdy flower stalks emerge, up to 19 inches (50 cm) tall, dies back in fall; leaves stiffly upright, long, lanceolate, dark green to grass green
Location: Warm and bright, but not sunny; in summer, also outdoors
Care: Keep moderately damp; mist quite often; starting in spring, feed every two weeks until bloom; if leaves start to wilt after bloom, gradually reduce watering; after dieback and during dormancy, keep dry and dark at 59–64°F (15–18°C); propagate by dividing rhizomes
Use: Eye-catching plant for bright, warm rooms

Growth form:
Herbaceous perennial
Flowering period:
Sept.–April

Cyclamen persicum

Cyclamen

Other names: Persian violet
Family: Primrose (*Primulaceae*)
Origin: Forests and clumps of bushes in southern and southeastern Europe, North Africa
Flowers: Folded-back pink, red, violet, or white, also bicolored petals, September–April
Appearance: Compact-growing tuberous plant; flower stalk up to 8 inches (20 cm) long, towering above leaves; leaves are large, heart-shaped, dark green with silvery white marking
Location: All year round, bright and cool, ideally at 61°F (16°C); short-lived at higher temperatures
Care: During bloom, keep root ball well dampened, but never pour water directly on the tuber or rot may develop; ideally, water from below and quickly tip out any water remaining in the saucer; feed every two weeks during growth period; remove old leaves and stalks at the base
Use: For airy, cool rooms; often sold as seasonal plant from September on; usually discarded after flowering
Note: All parts of the plant are poisonous.

Growth form:
Herbaceous perennial
Flowering period:
Jan.–June

Cymbidium Hybrids
Cymbidium Orchids

Family: Orchid (*Orchidaceae*)
Origin: East Asia, Southeast Asia, Australia
Flowers: White, yellow, pink, reddish, brown, or greenish, often with contrasting lip; in long, panicled inflorescences; usually January–June
Appearance: Onion-shaped pseudobulbs with three leaves each, upright to overhanging; miniature hybrids up to 27 inches (70 cm); leaves long, straplike, light green
Location: Very bright, also sunny, but no blazing midday sun; humid air; all year round, keep warm by day (about 68°F [20°C]) but cooler at night if possible; during winter, night-time temperatures of 50–59°F (10–15°C), for miniature hybrids 59°F (15°C)
Care: Water amply in growth period and mist quite often, with low-lime, room-temperature water; until late summer, supply with orchid food every four weeks; water with more restraint during winter
Use: Miniature hybrids especially suitable for indoor use

Growth form:
Herbaceous perennial
Flowering period:
Spring or early summer

Dendrobium Species and Hybrids

Dendrobium Orchids

Family: Orchid (*Orchidaceae*)

Origin: Asia, Pacific Islands, Australia

Flowers: Large, often colored white and purple with darker spots (*D. nobile* and cultivars), hybrids (→ photo) also in many others colors ranging all the way to yellow; bloom in spring or early summer

Appearance: Epiphytic in nature; rhizomes with slender or thickened pseudobulbs, depending on species; leaves are lanceolate, leathery or soft

Location: Very bright, but no direct sun from April to August; warm, humid air; dormant period begins in fall, then cooling off to 50°F (10°C) is important at night, in winter even cooler

Care: Keep evenly and slightly damp, mist a little and often, always using lime-free water; fertilize sparingly every two to three weeks; water less in fall and stop feeding; keep almost dry during winter

Use: Flowering plant for bright locations

Growth form:
Shrub
Flowering period:
Nov.–March

Euphorbia pulcherrima

Poinsettia

Family: Spurge (*Euphorbiaceae*)
Origin: Tropical regions of Mexico
Flowers: Inconspicuous, surrounded by large, splendidly colored or white bracts; November–March
Appearance: Bushy growth, heavily branching; leaves are broad and ovate, often lobed to toothed, large, dark green
Location: Bright, at about 64°F (18°C)
Care: From May to November, keep only slightly damp, mist occasionally, and fertilize every two weeks; after bloom, shorten stems to about 6 inches (15 cm), then keep dry and cooler, at 53–59°F (12–15°C); when growth resumes, repot and put in a warmer spot again. Flowers and bracts form only if plants spend 14 hours in total darkness at night for two months; cover with bucket or cardboard box in early evening
Use: For bright rooms; usually grown only as a seasonal plant and discarded after bloom
Note: All the parts are poisonous.

Growth form:
Annual
Flowering period:
July–Aug.

Eustoma grandiflorum

Prairie Gentian ✿

Other names: Lisianthus, Texas bluebell, tulip gentian
Family: Gentian (*Gentianaceae*)
Origin: Grasslands of southern U.S.A., northern Mexico
Flowers: Bell-shaped to deep cup-shaped; violet, blue, red, pink, or white; single or in clusters; unfolding in July–August from slender buds
Appearance: Grows bush and kept compact by growth retardants; leaves are ovate to oblong, bluish green
Location: Bright, if at all possible, but not in full sun; warm
Care: Keep moderately damp, avoid waterlogging at all costs; feed every two to three weeks in growth period; not worth cultivating after bloom finishes; propagate from seed in July–August (light germinator), 72–75°F (22–24°C) germination temperature essential; overwinter seedlings in bright, cool spot, and the next March put young plants in 4½-inch (12-cm) diameter pots, three to a pot; pinch out young plants often to promote bushy growth
Use: Striking seasonal plant for bright rooms

Growth form: *Biennial*
Flowering period: *July–Sept.*

Exacum affine

Persian Violet

Other names: German violet, Mexican violet
Family: Gentian (*Gentianaceae*)
Origin: Sokotra Island in the Indian Ocean
Flowers: Profusion of small, bowl-shaped flowers; blue, violet, pink, or white, with striking yellow stamens; July–September
Appearance: Upright, bushy, compact growth habit; leaves are small, ovate, shiny olive green
Location: Bright, but no direct sun; warm, well ventilated, in summer also outdoors
Care: Keep evenly damp, use lime-poor water; during the bloom, feed every two to three weeks; propagate from cuttings or from seed in February/March or in September (light generator, generation temperature of 64°F [18°C]); keep seedlings in a bright, cool spot all winter
Use: Pretty flowering plant for bright rooms; usually grown only as an annual

Growth form:
Shrub
Flowering period:
July–Oct.

Gardenia augusta

Gardenia

Other names: Cape jasmine; often sold also as *G. jasminoides*
Family: Madder (*Rubiaceae*)
Origin: Tropical forests of East Asia
Flowers: White, usually double, up to 4 inches (10 cm) across, fragrant
Appearance: Evergreen shrub, bushy; in a pot up to about 23½ inches (60 cm) tall; leaves are large, shiny dark green, leathery
Location: As bright as possible, but no direct sun; warm in summer; avoid sharp fluctuations in temperature and excess warmth during bud formation; in winter at 50–59°F (10–15°C)
Care: Keep evenly and slightly damp, using softened, room-temperature water; mist only before bloom; fertilize every two weeks with low-lime food and soil mix (such as rhododendron food and substrate); in fall, stop feeding and water with more restraint
Use: Magnificent flowering plant for bright, warm rooms and heated conservatories
Note: The fruit is poisonous.

Growth form:
Climbing plant
Flowering period:
June–Aug.

Gloriosa superba

Flame Lily

Other names: Glory lily, gloriosa lily, climbing lily
Family: Colchicum (*Colchicaceae*)
Origin: Tropical forests of Asia and Africa
Flowers: Lilylike, up to 3 inches (8 cm) across; initially green, then scarlet red with yellow margin; June–August
Appearance: Stems grow up to 6.5 feet (2 m) long, emerging from a tuberous root; leaves are lanceolate, glossy fresh green, with tendril-like tips
Location: Sunny; warm, humid air
Care: Keep evenly damp, avoid waterlogging; mist frequently, fertilize weekly; guide stems up climbing support; in fall, cease watering and feeding, and overwinter tubers in container at 59–64°F (15–18°C) in humid air; in spring, plant young tubers horizontally in fresh substrate, with growing tip about 1 inch (3 cm) below the surface
Use: For very bright, warm rooms, conservatories
Note: All parts of the plant (the tuber in particular) are very poisonous.

Growth form:
Herbaceous perennial
Flowering period:
Winter–late winter

Guzmania Hybrids

Guzmania ✿

Family: Bromeliad (*Bromeliaceae*)
Origin: Tropical forests of Central and South America
Flowers: Inflorescence with brilliant red to orange-red bracts; blooms primarily in late winter
Appearance: Grows as dense leaf rosette, from which a sturdy stalk emerges; leaves are long, glossy green, in some cases with decorative striping
Location: Bright to partial shade; warm and humid air
Care: Keep moderately damp with low-lime, room-temperature water; pour water also into the leaf funnel; mist often; feed lightly every two weeks; hard to propagate, as growing it from seed is time-consuming and offsets are uncommon
Use: For enclosed flower windows or warm rooms with high humidity
Note: The plants contain skin irritants.
Cultivars/Relatives: *G.* hybrids that stay small, such as 'Intermedia' and 'Magnifica,' are often sold (→ photo).

Growth form:
Bulb plant
Flowering period:
July–Oct.

Haemanthus albiflos

African Blood Lily

Other names: Royal paint brush
Family: Amaryllis (*Amaryllidaceae*)
Origin: Dry regions of South Africa
Flowers: Creamy white, in brushlike umbel on a sturdy stalk, with protruding yellow anthers; appearing in summer to late summer
Appearance: Evergreen bulb plant; stays compact with sessile leaves, above which the flower stalk rises in summer; leaves are broad and straplike, fleshy
Location: Sunny; warm in summer; during winter, bright and cool (about 50°F [10°C])
Care: Keep evenly and slightly damp, let soil surface dry out between waterings, and avoid waterlogging at all costs; during growth period, feed lightly every week; propagation by separation of offsets
Use: For bright rooms
Note: If the plant is kept too warm in the winter, the scapes (leafless flower stalks) tend to dry up.

Growth form:
Shrub
Flowering period:
March–Oct.

Hibiscus rosa-sinensis Hybrids

Hibiscus

Other names: Chinese hibiscus, rose of China
Family: Mallow (*Malvaceae*)
Origin: Tropical regions of East Asia
Flowers: Large, funnel-shaped, with long stamen tube; yellow, orange, red, pink, or white; March–October
Appearance: Grows as evergreen shrub; broad and bushy, up to about 6.5 feet (2 m) tall; can be trained as standard; leaves are ovate to heart-shaped, often with toothed margin, glossy dark green, in some cases also colored foliage
Location: As bright as possible, but no blazing sun; in summer, also outdoors in a sheltered spot; in winter, bright and cooler at 53–60°F (12–16°C)
Care: Keep evenly damp in growth period, and avoid waterlogging; in heated rooms, mist; feed weekly until August: remove faded blooms; leggy specimens must be cut back by one-half in spring
Use: Decorative indoor and container plant for bright locations, best as solitary specimen

Growth form: *Herbaceous perennial*
Flowering period: *Depends on cultivation*

Hippeastrum Species and Hybrids

Amaryllis

Other names: Dutch amaryllis
Family: Amaryllis (*Amaryllidaceae*)
Origin: Tropics and subtropics of Central and South America
Flowers: Funnel-shaped, up to 7 inches (18 cm); in many colors, also multicolored; from winter into spring, depending on when they were forced
Appearance: Bulb plant with upright, slightly drooping, straplike leaves and one to three leafless flower stalks
Location: Bright and warm during bloom and in main growth period, in summer also outdoors
Care: In winter, put bulb in water to half its height, in a warm place; do not water until the flower stalk is as tall as your hand; until mid-August, water and feed every two weeks; cut off withered leaves; during dormancy, keep bulb dark, cool, and dry
Use: Attractive decoration for bright, warm places
Note: All parts of the plant are poisonous.

Growth form: *Climbing shrub*
Flowering period: *May–Sept.*

Hoya bella

Wax Plant ✿

Family: Milkweed (*Asclepiadaceae*)
Origin: Tropical forests of Central Asia, Southeast Asia, and Australia
Flowers: Star-shaped, white or pale pink, waxy, sweetly scented; 7–12 inch (18–31 cm) umbels; May–September
Appearance: Twining climber with dense foliage, overhanging; leaves are narrow and ovate, succulent
Location: Bright and warm; in winter, not below 59°F (15°C)
Care: Keep evenly and slightly damp and fertilize every two weeks; mist occasionally; climbing support needed; in fall, water less, but don't let root ball dry out; to cut back, remove stems singly, leave short stalks in place after bloom so new buds can form
Use: Attractive climber, also suitable in hanging planters; for bright rooms; pretty as room divider
Cultivars/Relatives: *H. carnosa* is more opulent, cultivars have colored or wavy leaves; *H. kerrii* has cordate leaves and cream-colored flowers.

Growth form:
Shrub
Flowering period:
June–Aug.

Hydrangea Hybrids

Hydrangea

Family: Hydrangea (*Hydrangeaceae*)
Origin: Mountain forests of Japan and Korea
Flowers: Depending on cultivar, flowerheads are up to 7 ½ inches (20 cm) across; hemispheric, ball-shaped, or plate-shaped, umbels in pink, red, white, or blue on second-year wood; June–August
Appearance: Grows as deciduous shrub; broad and bushy, upright; leaves are large, ovate, coarsely toothed
Location: Bright, but no direct sun; cool (about 60°F [16°C]); well ventilated; in summer, shady; also outdoors; in winter, bright or dark at 35–46°F (2–8°C)
Care: Keep well dampened with lime-poor water, also pour water in saucer; until mid-August, provide rhododendron food weekly; after leaves drop in fall, reduce watering sharply; if needed, cut back in spring; propagate from tip cuttings
Use: For bright, cool rooms; as container plant
Note: Blue-flowering hydrangeas turn pink if the substrate is not acidic enough.

Growth form:
Herbaceous perennial
Flowering period:
All year round

Impatiens Hybrids

Impatiens ✿

Family: Balsam (*Balsaminaceae*)
Origin: East Africa, Asia, New Guinea
Flowers: Saucer-shaped, red, white, pink, bright pink, orange, or violet, also bicolored; single or double; almost all year round
Appearance: Bushy growth, 1–2 feet (30–60 cm) tall; leaves are elliptical and cordate, light or dark green, New Guinea impatiens hybrids often have pretty markings
Location: Bright, but not full sun, partial shade also suitable; in summer, also outdoors, sheltered from rain; overwinter in bright spot, *I. walleriana* hybrids at 50–59°F (10–15°C), New Guinea hybrids at 59–64°F (15–18°C)
Care: Always keep well dampened, but avoid waterlogging; during growth, feed lightly every two weeks; during bloom, water with restraint; propagation easy, from seed in January–March, or from tip cuttings; light germinator
Use: Uncomplicated flowering plant for rooms and balconies; usually grown as an annual
Note: The plant is mildly poisonous.

Ixora Species and Hybrids

Ixora

Family: Madder (*Rubiaceae*)

Origin: Tropical forests on the Indian subcontinent

Flowers: Four-lobed, in dense corymbs; in *I. coccinea* (→ photo) bright red; in *I.* hybrids also orange, salmon-color, or yellow; March–October

Appearance: Evergreen shrub, profusely branching; slow-growing, up to 3 feet (1 m); leaves are lanceolate and ovate, stiff, leathery, glossy green

Location: Bright, no direct sun; warm all year round, with 64–68°F (18–20°C) soil temperature; humid air, best on water-filled bed of gravel, no sudden temperature changes

Care: Water and mist regularly with lime-poor, room-temperature water; feed lightly every two weeks; do not move after buds form, to prevent flower drop later; in winter, keep somewhat drier; cut back after bloom to promote branching

Use: For flower windows or mini-greenhouses; warm, humid, bright rooms, conservatories

Growth form: *Climbing shrub*
Flowering period: *Depends on cultivation*

Jasminum polyanthum

Winter Jasmine

Family: Olive (*Oleaceae*)
Origin: Tropical Asia
Flowers: White inside, pink outside, narrow and tubular, starlike, in terminal clusters, in umbels; sweetly scented; blooming in different seasons, also possibly all year round in favorable conditions
Appearance: Climbing shrub with long, wiry, thin stems, evergreen; leaves are pinnate, glossy green
Location: Sunny and airy, in summer also outdoors in sheltered spot; in winter, bright, at 46–50°F (8–10°C); cool location stimulates flower production
Care: Keep slightly damp with lime-poor water; fertilize every two weeks; tie stems to climbing support; in winter, water less; cut back in spring or after bloom
Use: Graceful climber for rooms, balconies, patios, and conservatories
Cultivars/Relatives: True jasmine (*J. officinalis*) has white flowers and loses its leaves in fall.

Growth form:
Shrub
Flowering period:
Almost all year round

Justicia brandegeana

Shrimp Plant

Family: Acanthus (*Acanthaceae*)
Origin: Tropical forests of South and Central America
Flowers: White, in flower spikes formed by striking yellow or red bracts; almost all year round
Appearance: Shrubby growth, branching; leaves are about 2 inches (5 cm) long, ovate, dark green, with entire margins
Location: Bright, but no direct sun; warm; in summer, also outdoors; in winter, at least 54°F (12°C)
Care: Keep well dampened in summer, until August feed every two or three weeks; water sparingly in winter and cut back by one-third in spring
Use: Attractive in bright rooms and conservatories
Cultivars/Relatives: Brazilian plume flower (*J. carnea*): in summer, tubular pink to red flowers in spikelike inflorescence, mist occasionally and feed weekly until August; *J. rizzinii*: tubular yellow-red flowers in winter and spring, tolerates sun, in winter keep at 50–54°F (10–12°C) to promote flowering.

Growth form:
Herbaceous perennial
Flowering period:
Depends on cultivation

Kalanchoe blossfeldiana

Kalanchoe ✿

Family: Orpine or stonecrop (*Crassulaceae*)
Origin: Dry regions of Madagascar
Flowers: Dense cymes (false umbels) in red, yellow, orange, pink, bright pink, or white; blooms in winter and/or spring, with right management also all year round
Appearance: Upright, succulent herbaceous perennial; leaves are dark green, fleshy, elongated to oval with toothed margin
Location: Bright all year round, also sunny; in summer, warm; in winter cooler at above 59°F (15°C)
Care: In summer, water moderately, let substrate dry between waterings; in winter, keep almost dry, water more often if in warm spot; until August, feed every two weeks; removed faded parts, cut back hard after bloom to promote new growth
Use: Undemanding flowering plant for bright rooms; usually grown only as seasonal
Cultivars/Relatives: There are numerous cultivars, including mini-kalanchoe (about 6 inches [15 cm] tall).

Growth form:
Shrub
Flowering period:
May–June

Leptospermum scoparium

Tea Tree

Other names: Manuka
Family: Myrtle (*Myrtaceae*)
Origin: Humid, warm forests, principally in New Zealand and Australia
Flowers: Many tiny pink, red, or white flowers of five petals, single or double; May–June
Appearance: Grows as evergreen shrub, densely branching, can also be trained as standard; leaves needlelike, depending on cultivar green, blue-green, or bronze in color, with an aromatic scent when handled
Location: Bright, but no blazing sun; warm, in summer also outdoors; in winter at 39–46°F (4–8°C)
Care: Water generously with soft water in summer, but avoid waterlogging at all costs, as it leads to leaf drop and dryness; until August, feed every two weeks, using rhododendron food and substrate; after the bloom, thin out and cut back slightly
Use: For bright, warm rooms, as container plant

Growth form:
Climbing shrub
Flowering period:
June–Sept.

Mandevilla laxa

Chilean Jasmine

Other names: Mandevilla vine
Family: Dogbane (*Apocynaceae*)
Origin: Tropical forests of South America
Flowers: Five-petaled, white, funnel-shaped, scented; in terminal racemes on new stems; early summer–fall
Appearance: Grows as deciduous twining plant, fast-growing; leaves are ovate, shiny dark green, opposite
Location: Sunny and warm; in winter bright or dark and cool, at 39–46°F (4–8°C)
Care: Water abundantly in summer; fertilize weekly until August; provide with stakes or trellis to climb; if overwintered in a dark place, cut back stems to just above soil surface and keep plant almost dry
Use: Pretty flowering plant for bright rooms, conservatories, balconies, and patios
Note: The plant contains toxins; its aromatic substances can cause headaches.

Growth form:
Shrub
Flowering period:
March–Aug.

Medinilla magnifica

Showy Medinilla

Family: Black mouth plants (*Melastomataceae*)

Origin: Tropical forests of the Philippines

Flowers: Pink flowers in pendulous panicles up to 19 inches (50 cm) long, surrounded by large, pinkish white bracts; spring to summer

Appearance: Grows as evergreen shrub with tetragonal stems, up to 3 feet (1 m) tall; leaves are up to 1½ inches (30 cm) long, leathery, ovate-oblong

Location: Bright, no direct sun; warm (soil) and humid air, no drafts; at 59–64°F (15–18°C) from November until buds start to form; sensitive to change in location

Care: Once buds appear, keep evenly and slightly damp; water and mist with soft water only; until fall, feed with low-lime mix every two weeks; water very sparingly during dormancy

Use: Elegant flowering plant for enclosed flower windows and warm, humid conservatories

Growth form:
Herbaceous perennial
Flowering period:
Depends on species and cultivar

Miltonia Hybrids

Miltonia Orchids

Family: Orchid (*Orchidaceae*)
Origin: Tropical forests of South America
Flowers: Large and shallow, resembling pansies or violets; depending on cultivar, in widely varying colors, often white with pink and red, bicolored, or multicolored patterns; flowering period almost all year round, depending on species and cultivar
Appearance: Epiphyte; egg-shaped pseudobulbs with two leaves each; forms with only one leaf are also listed as *Miltoniopsis*; leaves usually long and narrow
Location: Bright to partially shady, no direct sun; humid air; by day in summer at 64–71°F (18–22°C), in winter at 59–64°F (15–18°C), at night somewhat cooler
Care: Keep evenly damp, but not wet, with lime-poor water; in winter, water sparingly; mist only surrounding air, not plants directly; in spring and summer, fertilize lightly with orchid food; propagate by division
Use: Good for east- and west-facing windows

Growth form:
Shrub
Flowering period:
May–Aug.

Nematanthus 'Glabra'

Goldfish Plant

Other names: Clog plant; in some cases still known by its old botanical name, *Hypocyrta glabra*
Family: Gesneriad (*Gesneriaceae*)
Origin: Tropical forests of Brazil
Flowers: Small, orange-yellow, with pouched, puffy-looking corolla tube and "mouth-like" tip; spring to late summer
Appearance: Grows as small, bushy shrub, slightly pendulous as it ages; leaves are elliptical, shiny dark green, fleshy
Location: As bright as possible, but no full sun; moderately warm, also outdoors in summer; a somewhat cooler location (around 59°F [15°C]) in winter stimulates flower production
Care: In summer, keep moderately damp with lime-poor water and fertilize every two weeks; shorten stems after bloom to promote new growth; water sparingly in winter
Use: Appealing bloomer for bright rooms; also pretty in hanging planters on the patio

Growth form:
Herbaceous perennial
Flowering period:
Summer

Neoregelia carolinae

Blushing Bromeliad

Family: Bromeliad (*Bromeliaceae*)
Origin: Tropical forests of Brazil
Flowers: Flat inflorescence; violet, surrounded by brilliant red inner leaves; summer
Appearance: Grows as flat, broad rosette; leaves are narrow, abruptly pointed; in cultivars often with multicolored markings, 'Tricolor' with green and white, some pink stripes; inner leaves turn red during bloom
Location: Very bright, but no direct sun; warm and humid all year round, best on gravel in water-filled bowl; cooler location (at 54–57°F [12–14°C]) after inner leaves change color prolongs life span
Care: Keep moderately damp and mist, using lime-poor, room-temperature water; always keep the inside of the rosette (cistern) full of water; fertilize every two weeks; propagate from offsets
Use: Decorative flowering and foliage plant, especially good in enclosed flower windows

Growth form: *Herbaceous perennial*
Flowering period: *April–May*

Nertera granadensis

Pincushion Plant

Other names: Bead plant
Family: Madder (*Rubiaceae*)
Origin: Tropical forests of Central and South America, Oceania
Flowers: Greenish, inconspicuous, turning into numerous orange-red pea-sized berries that last several months; April–May
Appearance: Grows as herbaceous perennial; low and cushion-like; leaves are very tiny, broad oval, fleshy
Location: Bright, but not in blazing sun; before and after bloom at 50–55°F (10–13°C), cool and humid; in summer, outside in sheltered spot; usually grown only as an annual
Care: Water only from the bottom to prevent rot; use stale water to which some liquid fertilizer is added every two weeks; mist often, but not during bloom; keep drier in winter
Use: For narrow window ledges and side tables
Note: The plant's berries are poisonous.

Growth form:
Herbaceous perennial
Flowering period:
Summer

Nidularium Species

Bird's Nest Bromeliad

Family: Bromeliad (*Bromeliaceae*)
Origin: Tropical forests of Brazil
Flowers: Branching inflorescence with colored bracts surrounded by eye-catching, colorful leaf areas at the center of the rosette; the prevalent species *N. fulgens* has blue-violet flowers and brilliant red rosette center; summer
Appearance: Broad funnel-shaped rosette; leaves are about 11½ inches (30 cm) long, broad-lanceolate; in *N. fulgens* with dark spots, in *N. innocentii* var. *lineatum* striped with yellow
Location: Bright; all year round at no less than 64°F (18°C), humid air
Care: Keep well dampened with lime-poor, room-temperature water; especially in summer, pour water also into leaf funnel; in winter, water less; during growth period, fertilize lightly every two weeks, also spray leaves with fertilizer solution; dry leaf tips caused by overly low humidity; propagate from offsets
Use: In a warm bathroom; ideal in enclosed flower window or mini-greenhouse

Growth form: *Herbaceous perennial*
Flowering period: *Depends on species and cultivar*

Oncidium Species and Hybrids

Oncidium Orchids

Family: Orchid (*Orchidaceae*)
Origin: Tropical forests of Central and South America
Flowers: Usually small and profuse in long panicles; the individual flowers are yellow, white, pink, red, and brown, frequently banded or checkered (*Oncidium* hybrids → photo); callus situated at the base of the lip
Appearance: Epiphyte; pseudobulbs often egg-shaped; one or two leaves, long and narrow
Location: Bright to partly shady; humid air, warmth-tolerant species (such as *O. bicallosum, O. carthagenense*) at 68–77°F (20–25°C) by day, 60–64°F (16–18°C) at night; species for cool locations (such as *O. ornithorhynchum*) at 68–77°F (20–25°C) by day in summer, in winter at 64–71°F (18–22°C), markedly cooler at night
Care: In summer, water carefully with lime-poor, room-temperature water; mist frequently; in winter, water summer bloomers sparingly; during growth period, add orchid food every three weeks; propagate by division
Use: For window ledges and flower windows

Growth form: *Herbaceous perennial*
Flowering period: *Depends on species and cultivar*

Paphiopedilum Species and Hybrids

Lady's Slipper Orchids

Other names: Venus's slipper orchid
Family: Orchid (*Orchidaceae*)
Origin: Tropical forests of East Asia and Southeast Asia
Flowers: White, yellow, reddish, brown, or green, often striped or spotted; lip resembles slipper
Appearance: Usually lacks pseudobulbs; rosette-like, each with two to four leaf pairs; leaves are strap-like, fleshy, frequently with light spots or marbling
Location: Bright to part shade; in summer usually at up to 86°F (30°C), in winter not below 64°F (18°C)
Care: Water with soft, room-temperature water, let substrate dry out between waterings; don't pour water into "heart" or onto leaves; mist quite often; in winter keep slightly damp; in growth period supply with orchid food every two weeks
Use: For warm places without direct sun
Note: The plant contains toxins.
Cultivars/Relatives: Commercially available hybrids (→ photo) are usually somewhat more robust.

Growth form: *Climbing shrub*
Flowering period: *June–Sept.*

Passiflora caerulea

Blue Passion Flower

Family: Passion flower (*Passifloraceae*)
Origin: Tropical and subtropical South America
Flowers: Flat blooms as large as 4 inches (10 cm) across, with three stigmas surrounded by white sepals and petals and a corona of violet-white-blue, fleshy filaments; spring to fall
Appearance: Grows as perennial twining shrub, up to 6.5 feet (2 m); leaves are large, multilobed, dark green, with spiraling tendrils
Location: Very bright, but no blazing midday sun; in summer also outdoors; in winter, bright, at 43°F (6°C)
Care: Water abundantly in summer; fertilize weekly until August; guide stems loosely on stakes or rings in a pot or on a climbing frame; cutting back promotes new growth and flower production; propagate from tip cuttings, seed
Use: Climber for bright rooms and conservatories
Note: All parts of the plant except the fruit contain toxins.
Cultivars/Relatives: There are several similar species and hybrids, such as the edible *P. edulis* (purple passionfruit).

Growth form:
Shrub
Flowering period:
Sept.–May

Pavonia multiflora

Brazilian Candles

Other names: Botanically, also *Triplochlamys multiflora*
Family: Mallow (*Malvaceae*)
Origin: Tropical forests of Brazil
Flowers: Long stamens and pistil rise above a purple calyx surrounded by large, bright red bracts; September–May
Appearance: Evergreen shrub, usually kept compact by growth inhibitors but becoming leggy when their effect diminishes; leaves are large, lanceolate, dark green
Location: Very bright, but no blazing sun; warm and humid air; in winter around 64°F (18°C)
Care: Keep moderately damp with lime-poor water; water even less in winter, mist often if air is dry; in summer, feed every two weeks; cut back after bloom; propagate from tip cuttings at 86–95°F (30–35°C) (difficult)
Use: Pretty winter bloomer for bright rooms, also attractive in conservatories

Growth form:
Subshrub
Flowering period:
March–July

Pelargonium grandiflorum Hybrids

Regal Pelargonium

Other names: Commonly known as "geranium"
Family: Cranesbill (*Geraniaceae*)
Origin: Original species primarily from South Africa
Flowers: Red, pink, violet, white, also bicolored; single or double; in long-stemmed, umbel-like inflorescences
Appearance: Bushy, upright, partially lignifying subshrubs; leaves are stemmed, large, rounded to kidney-shaped, sinuate, toothed, or lobed, in some cases with striking markings or margins
Location: Bright but not sunny, in summer also outdoors, in winter at 50–59°F (10–15°C)
Care: Keep well dampened, but avoid waterlogging; feed every two weeks until August; deadhead regularly; cut back lightly after bloom, then repot; propagate from tip cuttings at about 54°F (12°C), not warmer, or flowering will decrease
Use: Attractive plant for indoors, has only limited use on balconies and patios because of early bloom time

Growth form:
Subshrub
Flowering period:
Sept.–Jan.

Pentas lanceolata

Egyptian Star Cluster

Family: Madder (*Rubiaceae*)
Origin: Tropical Africa and Arabia
Flowers: Pink, red, violet, or white, up to 1 inch (3 cm) long, narrow funnel-shaped blooms in stemmed, terminal clusters of false umbels; September–January
Appearance: Bushy, branching subshrub; leaves are lanceolate, light green, with soft shoots and covered with fine hair
Location: Sunny; warm and humid air, but well ventilated; in summer also outdoors; in winter at 54–59°F (12–15°C)
Care: In growth period, keep well dampened but avoid waterlogging; feed weekly; in winter, water less. The plants usually are treated with growth retardants; when the effect lessens, growth is increasingly leggy, so trim stems frequently; propagate from tip cuttings at soil temperature of 68–77°F (20–25°C), or from seed (light germinator); pinch back young plants several times
Use: Winter-blooming plant for bright rooms, conservatories with the right temperature, and greenhouses

Growth form:
Herbaceous perennial
Flowering period:
Varies

Phalaenopsis Hybrids

Moth Orchids

Other names: Phalaenopsis hybrids
Family: Orchid (*Orchidaceae*)
Origin: Tropical forests of Asia, Australia, Oceania
Flowers: Mothlike; white, pink, or pale violet; more demanding species grown by fanciers also yellow, red, purple, and multicolored; flowering time varies by cultivar
Appearance: Usually epiphytic; no pseudobulbs, but fleshy roots producing leaves from the top and very long panicles of flowers; leaves are broad, leathery, dark green, sometimes spotted
Location: Bright to partially shady; humid air; by day at 68–77°F (20–25°C), at night at minimum of 60°F (16°C)
Care: Keep moderately damp with lime-poor, room-temperature water, let substrate dry between waterings; don't pour water into "heart" or on leaves; mist often; supply with orchid food every two weeks
Use: The hybrids are low-maintenance, highly attractive bloomers for spots with no direct sun

Growth form:
Herbaceous perennial
Flowering period:
Jan.–May

Primula Hybrids
(*P. vulgaris* and *P. elatior* Hybrids)
Primrose

Family: Primrose (*Primulaceae*)
Origin: Forests and meadows in Asia and Europe
Flowers: Common primrose (*P. vulgaris* hybrids) early in spring, has short-stemmed flowers in almost all colors; oxlip primroses from March to May, with flower rosettes on sturdy stems, mostly in shades of yellow
Appearance: Low-growing, with leaf rosettes; leaves are oval to heart-shaped
Location: Bright or partly shady, no blazing sun; best in cool temperatures of roughly 50–59°F (10–15°C)
Care: Keep evenly and well dampened, but avoid waterlogging; during bloom, feed lightly every two weeks; propagate from seed (but difficult; common primrose is a light germinator)
Use: For cool rooms; pretty as table decoration or on narrow windowsills; primroses are usually grown as seasonal plants and discarded after bloom; can be planted outside in the garden

Growth form:
Herbaceous perennial
Flowering period:
Jan.–May

Primula obconica

German Primrose

Family: Primrose (*Primulaceae*)

Origin: Forests and meadows in Asia

Flowers: From Christmas until far into spring, large flowers in scented clusters on firm stalks; depending on cultivar, white, pink, or lilac

Appearance: Dense leaf rosette; leaves are oval

Location: Bright or partially shady, no blazing sun; best at cool temperatures of around only 50–59°F (10–15°C)

Care: Keep evenly and well dampened, but avoid waterlogging; during bloom, feed lightly every two weeks; propagate from seed (but difficult)

Use: For cool rooms; pretty as table decoration or on narrow windowsills; usually grown as seasonal plant and discarded after bloom

Note: Because it contains the toxin primin, which can trigger skin irritations and allergies, the plant often is called the "poison primrose." When buying, look for new, primin-free cultivars.

Growth form:
Shrub
Flowering period:
Nov.–May

Rhododendron simsii Hybrids

Indoor Azalea

Other names: Formosa azalea
Family: Heather (*Ericaceae*)
Origin: Forests of China and Japan
Flowers: White, pink, red, or violet; single or double; in umbel-like racemes; November–May
Appearance: Evergreen shrub; spreading and bushy, also grows as standard; leaves are ovate to lanceolate, glossy dark green, leathery
Location: Bright to partly shady; moderately warm and humid; in summer also outdoors; in fall as cool as possible, at 41–59°F (5–15°C), after buds appear at about 64°F (18°C)
Care: Keep evenly damp with lime-poor water, avoid waterlogging and dry root ball at all costs; mist occasionally; feed weekly in growth period and break off faded inflorescences; to repot use only special soil mix
Use: For cool rooms and conservatories
Note: All parts of the plant contain toxins.

Growth form:
Dwarf shrub
Flowering period:
June–Oct.

Rosa Species and Hybrids

Rose

Family: Rose (*Rosaceae*)
Origin: Very old cultigen; original forms from East Asia, Europe
Flowers: In Chinese rose (*Rosa chinensis* 'Minima' → photo), red; other miniature and dwarf roses in almost all colors but blue; June–October
Appearance: Bushy, deciduous, summer-blooming dwarf shrubs; leaves are unpaired and pinnate, with five or seven ovate, toothed leaflets, shiny
Location: Sunny and airy, with no heat build-up, in summer best outdoors; in winter, bright at about 41°F (5°C); to promote bloom, put in a warmer place as of February
Care: Water regularly in growth period, avoiding waterlogging; drier in winter; feed every two weeks until late July; deadhead regularly; cut back in early spring
Use: For bright, sunny rooms, patios, balconies
Note: Indoors, often keeps for only one year.

Growth form:
Herbaceous perennial
Flowering period:
All year round

Saintpaulia ionantha Hybrids

African Violet ✿

Family: Gesneriad (*Gesneriaceae*)
Origin: Original species from forests of East Africa
Flowers: Five-lobed, short-stemmed single flowers in bunchy inflorescence; pink, red, violet, blue, and white, also multicolored; all year round
Appearance: Compact growth with dense leaf rosette; leaves are rounded to oval, dark green on top; fleshy, with covering of fine hair
Location: Bright, but no direct sun, also good in part shade; warm, dislikes "cold feet," in winter not below 64°F (18°C)
Care: Keep moderately damp with soft, room-temperature water; don't get leaves wet, but water right under leaf rosette or in saucer, avoiding waterlogging at all costs and keeping slightly drier in winter; feed lightly every two weeks in growth period; pluck off wilted blooms and leaves regularly; propagate from tip cuttings at soil temperature of 68–77°F (20–25°C)
Use: Pretty decoration for warm rooms

Growth form:
Annual
Flowering period:
July–Oct.

Schizanthus wisetonensis Hybrids

Poor Man's Orchid

Other names: Butterfly flower
Family: Nightshade (*Solanaceae*)
Origin: Original species native to Chile
Flowers: Large, asymmetrical flowers in clustered inflorescence; white, yellow, pink, red, violet, often spotted or veined; July–October
Appearance: Grows as an annual; leaves are pinnate, light green; soft
Location: Bright to sunny; warm and airy, in summer also outdoors in sheltered spot
Care: Always keep damp, but not wet; fertilize weekly; deadhead regularly to promote renewed flowering; propagate from seed from February to April at 60–64°F (16–18°C); or from seed in fall (overwinter plants at 50°F [10°C]), then bloom begins in April
Use: Adds colorful accent in rooms or on balconies
Note: The plant contains toxins. It is usually only grown indoors as an annual.

Growth form:
Herbaceous perennial
Flowering period:
May–July

Scutellaria costaricana

Scarlet Skullcap

Family: Mint (*Lamiaceae*)
Origin: Tropical forests of Costa Rica
Flowers: Orange-red to red tubular flowers with yellow throats, in terminal spikes; May–July
Appearance: Bushy herbaceous perennial with red-brown stems, up to 15 inches (40 cm) tall; leaves are large, oval with pointed tips, dark green, opposite
Location: As bright as possible, no direct sun; in growth period warm, in winter not below 59°F (15°C)
Care: Keep moderately damp at all times, avoid dry root ball and waterlogging; from spring to fall feed weekly, in winter only monthly; most plants are treated with growth retardants and become leggy over time as effect lessens, and regular cutting back after bloom helps prevent this; propagate from tip cuttings in fall
Use: On windowsill in bright, warm rooms and in flower windows

Growth form:
Herbaceous perennial
Flowering period:
All year round

Sinningia Hybrids

Gloxinia

Family: Gesneriad (*Gesneriaceae*)
Origin: Tropical forests of Brazil
Flowers: Numerous hybrid cultivars with diverse, bell-shaped, tubular, or trumpet-shaped large or small flowers, single or double; white, pink, red, violet, or blue, often marked with spots or dots; at all seasons
Appearance: Rhizome-producing herbaceous perennial with leaves in rosette-like arrangement; leaves are felted and soft, often furrowed, large, ovate, medium to dark green
Location: Bright all year round, but no direct sun; warm and humid
Care: Keep well dampened with soft, room-temperature water; feed weekly; keep surrounding air humid, don't mist leaves directly; propagate from leaf cuttings or by rhizome division, keep pieces in damp sand at 77°F (25°C)
Use: Magnificent bloomer for bright rooms with humid air
Note: Hybrids are often available as seasonal plants.

Growth form:
Shrub
Flowering period:
May–June

Solanum pseudocapsicum

Jerusalem Cherry Plant

Family: Nightshade (*Solanaceae*)
Origin: Island of Madeira in Atlantic Ocean
Flowers: Greenish white, May–June; in summer becoming
spherical, long-lasting berries, first green, then yellow,
and finally coral-red; in some cultivars also golden yellow
('Goldball') or white before turning red ('Snowfire')
Appearance: Grows as shrub about 11½ inches (30 cm) tall;
leaves are small, dark green, leathery
Location: Bright, also sunny; not too warm (about 59°F
[15°C]) and humid; in summer also outdoors
Care: In summer, water amply; feed every two weeks until fall;
to overwinter, cut back in fall and put in bright, cool spot, in
February raise temperature slightly to stimulate growth;
propagate from seed, pinch back young plants twice
Use: Decorative fruit-bearing plant for cool rooms
Note: All parts of the plant are poisonous. It is usually
available for sale in late summer as a seasonal plant.

Growth form: *Herbaceous perennial*
Flowering period: *Spring–summer*

Spathiphyllum Species and Hybrids

Peace Lily

Other names: White anthurium
Family: Arum lily (*Araceae*)
Origin: Tropical forests of America
Flowers: Towering white to cream-colored spadix, surrounded by a large white spathe; spring–summer
Appearance: Grows in clumps, with leaves arising in clusters from short stem; leaves are large, lanceolate, shiny green, long-stemmed
Location: Bright to partly shady; warm and humid all year round
Care: In summer, keep moderately damp, mist occasionally (using lime-poor, room-temperature water); feed lightly every week from spring to fall; water less in winter
Use: Unusual, elegant foliage and flowering plant for warm rooms and conservatories
Note: All parts of the plant contain toxins.
Cultivars/Relatives: Besides commercially available *S.* hybrids (→ photo), *S. wallisii* also good for indoor culture.

Growth form:
Climbing shrub
Flowering period:
May–Aug.

Stephanotis floribunda

Madagascar Jasmine

Family: Milkweed (*Asclepiadaceae*)
Origin: Forests and clumps of bushes in Madagascar
Flowers: White, tubular, radiating and starlike at tip;
in loose umbels; intense scent; May–August
Appearance: Evergreen twining shrub with meter-long stems;
leaves are large, oval, glossy dark green, often with lighter
midrib
Location: Very bright, but no direct sun; airy; warm, at
64–71°F (18–22°C), cooler in winter (54–60°F [12–16°C])
Care: Water amply in spring and summer, mist regularly,
with soft, room-temperature water; until mid-August feed
every two weeks; tie stems to climbing support, cut back long
stems; in winter keep slightly damp; propagate from tip
cuttings at 77–86°F (25–30°C)
Use: Decorative flowers with marvelous scent, for bright
place on windowsill and in conservatory
Note: After buds have set, do not move or rotate. This will
help prevent bud drop.

Growth form: *Herbaceous perennial*
Flowering period: *May–Sept.*

Streptocarpus Species and Hybrids

Cape Primrose

Family: Gesneriad (*Gesneriaceae*)
Origin: Tropical Africa and Madagascar
Flowers: Long-stemmed, asymmetrical funnel-shaped flowers in loose inflorescences; white, pink, red, violet, or blue, sometimes with different-colored throat; spirally twisted fruit (botanical name!); May–September
Appearance: Usually grows as rosette; leaves are linear, wrinkled, with fine hairs
Location: Bright or partially shady; at 59–68°F (15–20°C)
Care: Always keep moderately damp, using soft, room-temperature water; in cool spot, water less; from March to August feed lightly each week
Use: For moderately warm rooms
Note: Milky sap can irritate skin of people with sensitivities.
Cultivars/Relatives: 'Domino' hybrids have leaves only ¼–1 inch (1–3 cm) long, but are far less fussy than the occasionally available unifoliate species, such as *S. wendlandii*.

Growth form:
Herbaceous perennial
Flowering period:
Spring–summer

Tillandsia cyanea

Pink Quill

Family: Bromeliad (*Bromeliaceae*)
Origin: Tropical and subtropical Americas
Flowers: Flattened, spike-like to fan-like inflorescences with reddish to violet bracts, between which blue flowers appear; blooming spring to summer, bracts remain attractive long after bloom finishes
Appearance: Grows dense rosettes of narrow, coarse, leathery, terminally pointed leaves; roots in soil
Location: Bright, but no blazing sun, warm and humid, in winter not below 59–64°F (15–18°C)
Care: Always keep slightly damp, mist surrounding air often, avoid overwatering (danger of rot); feed lightly every four weeks (one-half concentration); pot with orchid soil mix or special bromeliad substrate; propagate from offsets
Use: Exotic decoration for warm rooms, best in mini-greenhouses or in enclosed flower windows
Note: The plant contains toxins.

Growth form:
Herbaceous perennial
Flowering period:
All year round

Vriesea splendens

Flaming Sword

Family: Bromeliad (*Bromeliaceae*)
Origin: Tropical forests of Central and South America
Flowers: Flattened, long inflorescence with bright red bracts surrounding yellow solitary flowers; blooms all year round, mainly in summer
Appearance: Grows as funnel-shaped rosette; leaves arching, with crosswise bands of dark red
Location: Bright to partly shady; warm and humid
Care: Keep evenly damp with lime-poor, room-temperature water, mist often; in winter, water less; feed lightly every two weeks; propagate from large offsets
Use: Ideal in enclosed flower window
Note: The plant contains toxins. It can be tied to epiphyte stems or grown in pot.
Cultivars/Relatives: Numerous hybrid cultivars with red or yellow bracts and glossy green or striped and spotted leaves.

Growth form:
Herbaceous perennial
Flowering period:
Feb.–June

Zantedeschia aethiopica

Common Calla Lily

Family: Arum lily (*Araceae*)
Origin: Damp grasslands in South Africa
Flowers: Towering, yellowish spadix enclosed in a white, funnel-shaped bract; late winter to early summer
Appearance: Grows with a turnip-shaped rhizome from which upright leaves and flower stalks emerge, up to 31 inches (80 cm) tall; leaves are long-stemmed, large, arrow-shaped, lush green
Location: Bright to partially shady; during bloom around 68°F (20°C), in summer also outdoors; in fall and early winter at about 50°F (10°C), warmer again once flower stalk appears
Care: Water amply during bloom, then sparingly and from fall on scarcely at all; fertilize weekly in growth and flowering periods
Use: As solitary specimen in elegant surroundings
Note: The plant contains toxins.
Cultivars/Relatives: Hybrids have pastel or brilliantly colored bracts.

Foliage Plants
from A to Z

You don't need luxuriant, brightly hued flowers to create an attractive look— leaves in their many variations have charms of their own to offer. The wide assortment of ornamental foliage plants, ranging from majestic indoor trees to lacy dwarf plants, allows you to select the ideal plant for every situation.

A

Growth form:
Shrub

Acalypha wilkesiana Hybrids

Copperleaf

Other names: Joseph's coat, fire dragon
Family: Spurge (*Euphorbiaceae*)
Origin: Islands of the South Pacific
Appearance: Grows bushy, depending on cultivar, compact or to 6.5 feet (2 m) tall; leaves are large, with serrate margin, depending on cultivar, green, yellowish, pink, or red-brown, also multicolored
Location: Bright, but no full sun, in overly dark spot cultivars with colored leaves turn green; warm all year round
Care: Keep evenly damp but not wet; feed every two weeks, less often in winter; mist with lukewarm, soft water; propagate from tip cuttings in spring at soil temperature of no less than 68°F (20°C) and in high humidity
Use: Especially attractive in groups
Note: All parts of the plant are poisonous.
Cultivars/Relatives: 'Musaica' has bronze-red, patterned leaves; 'Marginata' has green leaves edged in pink; 'Godseffiana' has light green leaves with white margins.

Growth form: *Herbaceous perennial*

Acorus gramineus

Japanese Sweet Flag

Family: Sweet flag (*Acoraceae*)
Origin: Swampy regions in China, India, and Japan
Appearance: Grasslike, in dense clumps, with creeping rhizome; leaves are very narrow, stiffly upright to overhanging; cultivars with yellow-green or white-green striping
Location: Bright, green-leaved plants also in part shade; cool and airy, in summer best outdoors; in winter cold, but above freezing point
Care: In summer keep well dampened, never let root ball dry out; also tolerates water in saucer; fertilize every two weeks, in winter only occasionally
Use: Dainty-looking foliage plant for bright, cool stairwells and living spaces
Note: The rhizome is poisonous.
Cultivars/Relatives: The green-leaved cultivar 'Pusillus' grows no more than 4 inches (10 cm) tall. 'Variegatus' (→ photo), 'Ogon,' and 'Aureovariegatus' have yellow-striped leaves, and 'Albovariegatus' has white stripes on the leaves.

Growth form:
Herbaceous perennial

A

Adiantum Species

Maidenhair Fern

Other names: Venus-hair fern

Family: Maidenhair fern (*Adiantaceae*)

Origin: Rain forests of Central and South America

Appearance: Upright, bushy growth; *A. raddianum*
(→ photo) to 15 inches (40 cm); *A. tenerum* to 39 inches
(100 cm); leaves are finely pinnate fronds with thin, black
shining stems and dainty, wedge-shaped to rounded pinnae;
A. raddianum has almost triangular fronds, *A. tenerum*,
fan-shaped fronds

Location: Partially shady to shady; warm, at 68–77°F
(20–25°C), and humid; best in enclosed flower window
or on damp gravel bed; avoid drafts

Care: Keep evenly damp and mist surrounding air often,
using lime-poor, warmed water; feed lightly every two weeks;
propagate from spores at high soil temperature of 75–79°F
(24–26°C) or by division

Use: Appealing foliage plant for humid, warm, shady spots

Growth form: *Subshrub*

Aglaonema Species

Chinese Evergreen

Family: Arum lily (*Araceae*)
Origin: Rain forests of Southeast Asia
Appearance: *A. commutatum* (→ photo), the most common species, grows shrubby and upright, to 19 inches (50 cm) tall; *A. crispum*, to 3 feet (1 m); *A. costatum* usually procumbent; leaves are large, oblong, pointed, dark green, usually with white or silvery leaf spots
Location: Cultivars with colorful leaves, very bright but not sunny, those with green leaves, also part shade; warm all year round, in winter not below 59°F (15°C); best in humid, warm flower window or on damp gravel bed
Care: Keep moderately damp and mist often (with lime-poor, lukewarm water); feed lightly every two weeks, less often in winter; propagate by division in spring or from tip cuttings at soil temperature of at least 71°F (22°C) and in high humidity
Use: For humid locations, such as a bathroom
Note: All parts of the plant are poisonous.

Growth form:
Herbaceous perennial

Alocasia Species

Elephant Ear

Other names: Elephant's ear
Family: Arum lily (*Araceae*)
Origin: Tropical rain forests of Asia
Appearance: Erect with long-stemmed, sometimes pendent leaves; leaves are up to 15 inches (40 cm) long, arrow-shaped or shield-shaped, depending on species more or less with metallic shine; with white leaf vein on blue-green or dark green ground (*A. sanderiana* → photo, *A. lowii*) or dark-veined, light copper-colored leaves (*A. cuprea*)
Location: Partially shady; warm and humid, in winter not below 64°F (18°C)
Care: Keep evenly and slightly damp and mist quite often (with lime-poor, lukewarm water); water less in winter; feed lightly every two weeks; propagate from stolons or by division of rhizomes
Use: Best in enclosed flower windows; needs quite a lot of room
Note: The plant contains substances that can irritate mucous membranes.

Growth form:
Climbing shrub

Ampelopsis brevipedunculata

Amur Peppervine

Other names: Porcelain vine
Family: Grape (*Vitaceae*)
Origin: Forests of East Asia, primarily eastern China
Appearance: Long-stemmed, climbing; leaves are three-lobed, in *A. brevipedunculata* var. *maximowiczii* 'Elegans' (→ photo), suitable as a house plant, they are green-and-white checked, young plants faintly pink
Location: Bright, but not in blazing sun, also in part shade; in summer, also outdoors in warm spot, in winter bright and cool at 50–59°F (10–15°C)
Care: Water amply in summer, in winter keep almost dry; in growth period feed every two weeks; as climbing plant, it needs a support, so tie up stems; cut back in spring to promote bushy growth; propagate from tip or stem cuttings in summer
Use: Pretty as climber or in hanging planter at east- and west-facing windows, also good in conservatory
Note: The plant contains skin irritants.

Growth form:
Herbaceous perennial

Anthurium crystallinum

Crystal Anthurium

Family: Arum lily (*Araceae*)
Origin: Tropical rain forests of Central and South America
Appearance: Grows upright, leaf stalks to 15 inches (40 cm) long, with leaves hanging almost vertically from stalks; leaves are large, cordate, dark green, with white veining
Location: Bright to partially shady, no blazing sun; warm and humid, even in winter not below 64°F (18°C); soil temperature as warm as possible
Care: Keep moderately damp and mist quite often, using lime-poor, room-temperature water; feed every two weeks, less often in winter; propagate from tip or stem cuttings in warm, humid conditions, by air layering, or by division of older specimens
Use: Best in enclosed flower windows
Note: Anthuriums contain substances that can irritate skin or mucous membranes.
Cultivars/Relatives: *A. veitchii* has narrow, meter-long leaves with a white midrib and light side veins.

Growth form:
Conifer

Araucaria heterophylla

Norfolk Island Pine

Family: Araucaria (*Aracauriaceae*)
Origin: Forests of the Norfolk Islands (South Pacific)
Appearance: Trunk with symmetrically tiered horizontal branches; slow-growing, in indoor culture to 3–6.5 feet (1–2 m) tall; with dense-growing needles on frond-like branches; at first light green, in older specimens dark green; evergreen
Location: Bright, needs light from all sides to grow evenly; not too warm (best at 64°F [18°C]), in summer an outdoor stay is beneficial; in winter, bright, at 41–50°F (5–10°C)
Care: Keep evenly and slightly damp with lime-free water, drier in winter; mist often, especially in warm location; in summer, feed every two weeks with lime-poor fertilizer; propagate from cuttings taken from shoot tips, at a soil temperature of 77°F (25°C), high humidity and rooting hormone required (difficult)
Use: For bright, cool rooms, such as bedrooms

Growth form:
Palm

Areca catechu

Betel Nut Palm

Family: Palm (*Arecaceae, Palmae*)

Origin: Tropical rain forests of the Philippines

Appearance: Single-trunked, slender, slow-growing; leaves and fronds with broad-lanceolate, comb-shaped protruding leaflets; lush green; usually available as young plant with fronds still undivided, with V-shaped tips

Location: Bright to partially shady; warm and humid, even in winter not below 64°F (18°C)

Care: Keep well dampened, never let root ball dry out; with adequate soil temperature, a water-filled saucer is helpful; mist quite often; in summer, feed lightly every two weeks; propagate from seed at soil temperature of 77–86°F (25–30°C) (germination time: two to three months)

Use: Preferably for warm, humid conservatories and greenhouses, as young plant also for enclosed flower window; as house plant, somewhat fussy

Note: The nuts contain poisonous alkaloid in fairly high amounts.

Growth form:
Subshrub

Asparagus densiflorus

Asparagus Fern

Family: Asparagus (*Asparagaceae*)
Origin: Tropical and subtropical forests of Africa, Asia
Appearance: Shrubby plant with short trunk and in some cases heavily branching stems; long, arching stems; roots thickened and turniplike; side shoots appearing to be leaves; true leaves have developed into spines
Location: Bright, also sunny; warm in summer, cooler in winter, not below 54°F (12°C); in summer also outdoors
Care: Keep evenly and slightly damp, but avoid waterlogging; water less in winter; in warm location, mist occasionally; in growing season, feed once a week, in winter, once a month; propagate by division of the fleshy rhizome
Use: Pretty foliage plant with casual, debonair effect, attractive on columns beside large windows
Note: The red berries are poisonous.
Cultivars/Relatives: 'Sprengeri' has long, pendent stems; 'Myersii' is bushy, with stems like cats' tails.

Growth form:
Shrub

A

Asparagus falcatus

Sickle Thorn

Family: Asparagus (*Asparagaceae*)
Origin: Tropical and subtropical forests of Africa, Asia
Appearance: Shrubby, with meter-long climbing stems; sickle-shaped "leaves"; true leaves are absent or are small thorns; roots thickened and tuberous
Location: Bright, not sunny; in summer warm, in winter cooler, not below 54°F (12°C); in summer also outdoors
Care: Keep evenly and slightly damp, but avoid waterlogging; in winter, water less; in warm location, mist more often; in spring and summer, feed once a week, in fall and winter, once a month; propagate by division
Use: Elegant, filmy-looking foliage plant for large windowsills and conservatories; can also be grown as hanging plant
Cultivars/Relatives: *A. asparagoides* (bridal creeper, smilax) has broad, true leaves and also climbs.

Aspidistra elatior

Cast Iron Plant ✿

Other names: Iron plant, barroom plant
Family: Lily of the Valley (*Convallariaceae*)
Origin: Mountainous forests of China and Japan
Appearance: The leaves emerge from creeping rhizomes; occasionally, violet flowers appear near the ground on the new growth; leaves are evergreen; dark green, lanceolate, oblong, pointed; borne on long stalks to length of about 31 inches (80 cm) and width of 4 inches (10 cm); 'Milky Way' has white striping, 'Variegata' has creamy white to yellow stripes
Location: Bright to shady, but no direct sun; best cool, but can be kept warmer; in summer, also outdoors; in winter, cooler, not below 35°F (2°C); also tolerates dry air; keep striped cultivars in brighter, warmer places or they will turn green
Care: In summer, keep evenly damp, but avoid waterlogging; feed lightly once a month; propagate by division of rhizome
Use: Robust plant, also for stairwells and hallways

Growth form: *Herbaceous perennial*

Asplenium Species

Spleenwort

Family: Spleenwort (*Aspleniaceae*)

Origin: Tropical rain forests of Asia, Africa, and Australia

Appearance: *A. nidus*, the bird's nest fern (→ photo), forms a funnel-shaped rosette of leaves, as does *A. antiquum; A scolopendrium* (previously *Phyllitis scolopendrium*), the hart's tongue fern, grows in clusters. Leaves are large, undivided fronds, glossy green; cultivars also have incised or fringed fronds

Location: Bright to part shade; bird's nest fern and *A. antiquum*, warm, even in winter not below 64°F (18°C); hart's tongue fern, cool all year round

Care: Keep evenly damp with lime-poor water; mist often; in summer, feed lightly every two weeks

Use: Bird's nest fern and *A. antiquum* for warm, humid rooms or flower windows; hart's tongue fern for cool places

Note: The plants are sensitive to leaf-shine spray.

Growth form:
Herbaceous perennial

Begonia Species and Hybrids

Begonia

Family: Begonia (*Begoniaceae*)
Origin: Tropics and subtropics, except for Australia, cultivars
Appearance: Bushy, herbaceous, in some cases also pendulous; leaves asymmetrical, great variety of forms and colors; depending on species and cultivar, leaves are rounded with entire margins, lobed, serrate, or divided and in some cases long-stalked, diverse shades of green, brown to pink and red, often with very striking markings
Location: Bright, but no direct sun; from spring to winter, warm, in winter, cooler, not below 60°F (16°C)
Care: All year round, keep moderately damp with lime-poor water; high humidity required; don't mist leaves directly; feed every two weeks in growing season
Use: Attractive in bright rooms, also in hanging planters
Note: Some species contain substances that irritate mucous membranes.
Cultivars/Relatives: King or rex begonias (*B. rex* hybrids or *Rex cultorum* group, → photo) are popular.

Growth
form:
Tree

Brachychiton rupestris

Bottle Tree ✿

Other names: Queensland bottle tree
Family: Cocoa (*Sterculiaceae*)
Origin: Dry regions of Australia
Appearance: Grows as large tree in native habitat, but stays
small in a pot; trunk is thickened and bottle-shaped at base
(water storage), and above it rises a loosely branching crown;
over time the bizarrely shaped taproots emerge; leaves of
young specimens are fingered, older ones are simple and
lanceolate, evergreen
Location: Sunny to very bright and warm, in winter, cool, at
50°F (10°C) but well ventilated
Care: Water sparingly; feed every four to six weeks; cut back
in spring if needed; propagate from seed at 77°F (25°C),
scarify seed in advance
Use: Bonsai-like trees with unconventional nature, good
with succulent arrangements
Cultivars/Relatives: *B. populneus*, with lobed leaves,
is similar.

Growth form:
Palm

Brahea Species

Hesper Palm

Family: Palm (*Arecaceae, Palmae*)
Origin: Dry regions of California and Mexico
Appearance: Spreading, with thickened stem at base, slow-growing, *B. armata* (→ photo) can grow to 10 feet (3 m) in a container, *B. edulis* stays smaller, but grows broad; leaves are container large, rounded, stiff fronds; in *B. armata*, the blue hesper palm, silvery blue-green, in *B. edulis*, the Guadalupe palm, strong green
Location: Bright, also sunny; in summer also outdoors; tolerates dry air; overwinter at about 41°F (5°C), warmer if need be (maximum of 59°F [15°C])
Care: Keep only slightly damp, never wet; feed every two weeks in summer; needs pot with good drainage, best to mix some sand with substrate; propagate from seed; germination period at least two months
Use: Over time, a stately palm for large, bright rooms and conservatories; also as tub or container plant on balconies and terraces

Growth form: *Herbaceous perennial*

Caladium bicolor Hybrids

Caladium

Other names: Fancy-leafed caladium
Family: Arum lily (*Araceae*)
Origin: Cultivars, originally from the tropical forests of South America
Appearance: Leaves arise from a globose rhizome; leaves are large, thin with striking coloration, green, white, pink, or red spotted or marbled, borne on long stalks
Location: Bright to partially shady; high humidity, but don't mist leaves directly; as of September, water less and overwinter rhizome dry, at 64°F (18°C), after leaves drop; pot in spring, put in a bright, warm place and water; until August, feed every two weeks
Use: Best in enclosed flower window or in greenhouse
Note: The plant sap is a skin irritant.

Growth form:
Herbaceous perennial

Calathea makoyana

Peacock Plant

Other names: Brain plant
Family: Prayer plant (*Marantaceae*)
Origin: Tropical rain forests of South America
Appearance: Grows as herbaceous perennial; leaves borne on simple stalks of varying length, large, up to 19 inches (50 cm) long, oblong-oval; creamy ground color, irregularly spotted with dark green to brown-olive
Location: All year round, bright to partly shady, no direct sun; warm, humid air, in winter at about 59°F (15°C)
Care: In summer, keep evenly damp and mist often; in winter, water less; in summer, feed every two weeks, in winter, every four; propagate by division
Use: Very high-maintenance on window ledge, does best in flower window or conservatory
Note: With good local conditions, saffron-yellow flowers will appear.
Cultivars/Relatives: The leaves of *C. lancifolia* are crinkled. *C. majestica* has leaves with green-pink striping on top, red underneath.

Growth form:
Herbaceous perennial

Callisia Species

Roseling

Other names: *C. navicularis* also known as inch plant or Bolivian Jew

Family: Spiderwort (*Commelinaceae*)

Origin: Tropical rain forests of Central and South America

Appearance: *C. elegans, C. repens* (→ photo), and *C. navicularis* grow procumbent and creeping to pendent, *C. fragrans* more upright; leaves, depending on species and cultivar, uniform dark green or striped, in *C. fragrans* rosette-like, in *C. navicularis* boat-shaped on fleshy stems

Location: Bright to partly shady, brighter for cultivars with colored leaves, warm all year round, even in winter not below 60°F (16°C), humid air

Care: Keep evenly well dampened and mist generously with lime-poor water; in growth period, feed weekly, in winter every three to four weeks; propagate from cuttings under plastic hood

Use: As underplanting in conservatory, flower window, or greenhouse, also good in hanging planters

Growth form: *Herbaceous perennial*

Carex brunnea

Greater Brown Sedge

Other names: Sometimes listed also as *C. elegantissima*
Family: Sedge (*Cyperaceae*)
Origin: Grasslands of South Asia and Australia
Appearance: Grasslike, forms dense clumps, upright to slightly pendent; leaves very narrow, to 11½ inches (30 cm) long, with white striping
Location: Bright, but not in blazing sun, also partial shade; moderately warm, air not too dry; in winter at about 50°F (10°C)
Care: Keep evenly well dampened, but avoid waterlogging; mist surrounding air often; feed lightly once a month; propagate by division of older plants
Use: Pretty in wide bowls; suitable for bright rooms and conservatories
Cultivars/Relatives: The cultivar 'Variegata' has yellow stripes. Also good as a house plant is the related Japanese sedge, *C. morrowii*. It needs a shady, cool location and is kept somewhat drier.

Growth form:
Palm

Caryota mitis

Fishtail Palm

Family: Palm (*Arecaceae, Palmae*)
Origin: Southeast Asia, Malay Archipelago
Appearance: Multitrunked with slender stems, medium-sized; leaves are bipinnate fronds; leaflets triangular to wedge-shaped, resembling fishtails; dark green
Location: Bright, but not in blazing sun, also tolerates part shade if necessary; warm, best at 71–77°F (22–25°C), in humid air; even in winter not below 60°F (16°C)
Care: Keep well dampened with lime-poor, room-temperature water but avoid waterlogging; mist often; in summer, feed monthly; in cooler winter location, water less; propagate from seed or by division of clumps, high soil temperature required for raising from seed
Use: Unusual palm, which can be kept indoors with enough air humidity or frequent misting; thrives in damp, warm conservatories, greenhouses, or large, enclosed flower windows

Growth form:
Herbaceous perennial
Flowering period:
All year round

Ceropegia linearis ssp. *Woodii*

Rosary Vine

Other names: Collar of hearts, string of hearts
Family: Milkweed (*Asclepiadaceae*)
Origin: South Africa; Cape region to Zimbabwe
Appearance: Has long, thin stems up to 6.5 feet (2 m) in length, arising from a thickened, tuberous root; the plant produces small, flesh-colored flowers, resembling candles or candelabra, almost all year; leaves are small, fleshy, heart-shaped, light green on top with silvery white marbling, reddish beneath
Location: Sunny all year round; normal room temperature or warmer, in winter 54–59°F (12–15°C); in summer, also outdoors if sheltered from wind and rain
Care: In summer, keep only moderately damp, no waterlogging; in winter, water less; in summer, provide with cactus food every two weeks; propagate from brood tubers arising in leaf axils
Use: Low-maintenance, attractive plant for hanging planters

Growth form:
Palm
Flowering period:
All year round

Chamaedorea elegans

Parlor Palm ✿

Family: Palm (*Arecaceae, Palmae*)
Origin: Tropical regions of Central America
Appearance: Rather dainty, with slender trunk and slightly pendent fronds; even young plants produce yellow to cream-colored flowers all year round; dioecious, that is, separate male and female flowers grow on different specimens; leaves to 24 inches (60 cm) long, in fronds with lineal to lanceolate leaflets; fresh green
Location: Bright to partly shady; warm, about 68°F (20°C), and humid air, in summer also outdoors; in winter, put in cooler place, ideally at 54–59°F (12–15°C)
Care: In summer, keep well dampened but not waterlogged and feed every two weeks; mist occasionally; propagate from seed or sprigs
Use: Robust indoor plant, also good as container plant, and easy to cultivate in cool conservatory
Cultivars/Relatives: *C. metallica* has undivided leaves with metallic sheen and grows only about 3 feet (1 m) tall.

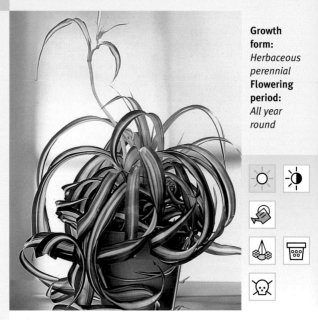

Growth form:
Herbaceous perennial
Flowering period:
All year round

Chlorophytum comosum

Spider Plant ✿

Other names: Spider ivy, ribbon plant
Family: Fringed lily (*Anthericaceae*)
Origin: Subtropical regions of South Africa
Appearance: Leaves borne in dense rosettes; on stems up to 3 feet (1 m) long, inconspicuous white flowers appear, later developing into numerous young plants; leaves are long, narrow, lineal, green, in the cultivar 'Variegata' with yellow or whitish stripes and in 'Curly Locks' (→ photo) twisted in spirals
Location: Bright to partly shady, warm all year round; in summer outdoors, sheltered from wind and rain
Care: Keep evenly well dampened, no waterlogging; in growth period, feed every two weeks; propagate by removing and cultivating plantlets
Use: Indoors, in hanging planters, atop columns; not good in arrangements because of vigorous root growth
Note: The seeds are poisonous.

Growth
form:
Palm

Chrysalidocarpus lutescens

Butterfly Palm

Other names: Areca palm, golden cane palm
Family: Palm (*Arecaceae, Palmae*)
Origin: Tropical forests of Madagascar
Appearance: The fronds are borne on thin trunklets that always grow in clusters and make the plant look luxuriant; leaves with comblike, pinnate, long fronds that hang over slightly; light green leaflets are borne on yellowish, dark-spotted leaf shafts
Location: Bright all year round, but no blazing sun; warm, even in winter not below 60°F (16°C), young plants not below 68°F (20°C); in summer also outdoors, in a sheltered spot
Care: In summer, always keep well dampened, in cooler location in winter, water less; mist frequently, especially in dry, heated air; in summer, feed every three to four weeks, in winter every six; propagate from seed or by removing and planting offsets
Use: Solitary specimen for indoors, conservatory, or green-house; also good container plant for patio

Growth form: *Climbing shrub*

Cissus discolor

Rex Begonia Vine

Other names: Climbing begonia, trailing begonia
Family: Grape (*Vitaceae*)
Origin: Tropical and subtropical regions of Southeast Asia, especially Java
Appearance: Climbing shrub; leaves are evergreen, cordate, purple-violet on top with light markings, reddish beneath
Location: Bright to partly shady, no blazing sun; warm all year round, 68–75°F (20–24°C) and humid air
Care: Keep evenly and slightly damp, but no waterlogging; mist amply all year round; in summer, feed every two weeks, otherwise every four weeks; plants need a climbing support such as a trellis, unless they are in a hanging planter or atop a pedestal; prune in late winter if needed
Use: Attractive in hanging planter or as climber, best in enclosed flower window
Cultivars/Relatives: *C. striata* (miniature grape ivy) has small, lobed leaves on striped stems.

Growth form: *Climbing shrub*

C

Cissus rhombifolia

Grape Ivy

Family: Grape (*Vitaceae*)

Origin: Tropics and subtropics of North and South America

Appearance: Climbing shrub; leaves are evergreen, three-lobed with long stalks, dark green and shiny, often with reddish hairs beneath, especially when young

Location: Bright to partially shady, no blazing sun; in winter between 60–64°F (16–18°C)

Care: Keep evenly and slightly damp, avoid waterlogging; in winter in a cool location, water only enough to keep root ball from drying out; mist amply all year round; in summer, feed every two weeks, otherwise every four weeks; proving climbing support if not in hanging planter; prune in late winter if necessary

Use: Attractive climber, also good in hanging planters indoors, in greenhouse, or in conservatory

Cultivars/Relatives: 'Ellen Danica' is a robust, low cultivar with three-part leaves; *C. antarctica* (kangaroo vine) has glossy, egg-shaped leaves.

Growth form:
Shrub

Clusia major

Strangler Fig

Other names: Often still listed as *C. rosea*
Family: Mangosteen (*Clusiaceae*)
Origin: Florida, West Indies, Mexico to northern South America
Appearance: Treelike or shrubby; leaves are evergreen, obovate and smooth-margined, dark green, shiny, leathery, resembling foliage of rubber tree
Location: Bright, but no direct sun; warm all year round, even in winter not below 64–68°F (18–20°C)
Care: Keep slightly and evenly damp with decalcified water and mist often; in summer, feed every two weeks with half-strength fertilizer
Use: Good-looking foliage plant with ornamental effect, pretty beside large windows
Note: Older specimens sometimes bear creamy white to light-pink, fragrant flowers.
Cultivars/Relatives: 'Marginata' and 'Aureo variegata' have variegated leaves.

**Growth
form:**
Palm

C

Cocos nucifera

Coconut Palm

Family: Palm (*Arecaceae*, *Palmae*)

Origin: Found in tropical regions worldwide

Appearance: In young plants, leaves are still connected to fruit; in natural habitat plants grow to 98 feet (30 m) tall; leaves are very long, pinnate, drooping fronds; bright, fresh green; however, only young coconut palms are commercially available, with as yet undivided, broad lanceolate leaves

Location: All year round, sunny to bright, needs additional artificial lighting in winter; warm, in winter tolerates down to 64°F (18°C) with enough light; humidity as high as possible

Care: Keep evenly damp, water less if in cooler location in winter, but never let root ball dry out; keep humidity high; in summer feed every four weeks, in winter, every two weeks

Use: Attractive solitary specimen, best in warm conservatory

Growth form:
Shrub

Codiaeum variegatum

Croton ✿

Other names: Garden croton
Family: Spurge (*Euphorbiaceae*)
Origin: Tropical forests of the Moluccas, cultivars
Appearance: Shrubby growth; leaves are evergreen, highly variable in shape: long, short, narrow, lobed, entire-margined, some twisted, leathery, glossy foliage in shades of green, yellow, orange, red to almost black, often also spotted, striped, veined, or dotted
Location: Bright, no direct sun; warm and humid all year round; sensitive to cold soil temperature and drafts
Care: In summer, keep evenly and slightly damp, drier in winter; mist often; use lime-poor water; feed lightly every two weeks; propagate by air layering; tip cuttings at high temperature (difficult)
Use: Very lively, colorful ornamental plant with no special needs
Note: Milky sap can cause allergic skin reactions. If the location is too dark, leaf coloration will be lost.

Growth form:
Shrub
Flowering period:
June–Aug.

Coffea arabica

Coffee Plant

Family: Madder (*Rubiaceae*)
Origin: Tropical mountainous forests of Africa
Appearance: Upright, shrubby, later leggy and outspreading; leaves are pointed oval, long, shiny green, and leathery; tiny white star-shaped flowers, fragrant, appear only on older specimens, June–August
Location: Bright, but not in blazing sun; warm and humid, in winter also cooler at 59°F (15°C)
Care: Water amply in summer, sparingly in winter, using only lime-free water; until August feed moderately every two weeks; mist often; propagate from tip cuttings or seed of fresh, unroasted coffee beans, which quickly lose their ability to germinate
Use: Interesting leaves and fruit; young specimens for bright windowsills, older ones for conservatories
Note: The cherry-sized, cherry-red fruit is very decorative.
Cultivars/Relatives: 'Nana' stays smaller and flowers even as a fairly young plant.

Growth form:
Shrub

Cordyline terminalis

Ti Tree

Other names: Hawaiian ti; also listed sometimes under old name *C. fruticosa*
Family: Agave (*Agavaceae*)
Origin: Tropical forests from Asia to Hawaii
Appearance: Roots grow thickened and clublike; over time a slender trunk forms, with a terminal tuft of leaves; leaves are broad-lanceolate to long-oval, to 19 inches (50 cm) long, stalked; cultivars' leaves are usually striped and/or spotted, from white through yellow and green to red
Location: Bright, no direct sun; warm all year round, even in winter not below 64°F (18°C); keep air as humid as possible
Care: Keep evenly damp; mist often; in summer feed weekly, in winter, every four weeks
Use: Green plant sculpture, best in enclosed flower window or conservatory
Cultivars/Relatives: The popular container plants *C. australis* and *C. indivisa* have long, narrow leaves.

Growth form:
Shrub

Corokia cotoneaster

Wire Netting Bush

Family: Escallonia (*Escalloniaceae*)
Origin: Forests and bush areas in New Zealand
Appearance: Small shrub; stems are dark, when young covered with downy hairs; they change growth direction when a new leaf appears, creating zigzagging effect; in late winter small, yellow flowers appear; deciduous, small, spatulate leaves, dark green on top, white-felted beneath
Location: Bright all year round, shelter from blazing midday sun; in summer best outdoors, protected from wind and rain, in winter, well-ventilated at about 41°F (5°C)
Care: In summer, keep slightly damp, in winter, water only sparingly; sensitive to waterlogging; in summer, feed lightly every four weeks; prune young plants often; propagate from cuttings that are not yet too woody
Use: Because of its bizarre growth habit, an unusual, graphically striking small shrub for cool room and a cold conservatory

Growth form: *Herbaceous perennial*
Flowering period: *March–Aug.*

Cryptanthus Species

Earth Star

Other names: Starfish plant
Family: Bromeliad (*Bromeliaceae*)
Origin: Tropical forests of South America
Appearance: Terrestrial bromeliad; plant forms low, star-shaped leaf rosettes; leaves are up to 4 inches (10 cm) long, coarse, some wavy, often with variegated stripes or bands; the tiny flowers are concealed inside the leaf rosette
Location: Bright, but no blazing midday sun; all year round at about 68°F (20°C)
Care: Keep slightly damp with lime-poor water; feed lightly every two weeks; mist often
Use: Good house plant if humidity is sufficient, otherwise better in enclosed flower window
Cultivars/Relatives: *C. bivittatus* has cultivars with pretty vertical striping on leaves, such as 'Tricolor' or 'Pink Starlight'; cultivars of *C. zonatus*, such as 'Zebrinus' (→ photo) have horizontal bands in various colors.

Growth form:
Tree
Flowering period:
All year round

Cycas revoluta

Sago Palm

Family: Cycad (*Cycadaceae*)
Origin: Forests on the southern Japanese islands
Appearance: From a short, thick trunk a new leaf crown appears roughly every 1–2 years; the plants are dioecious, that is, there are male and female plants; male flowers are cone-shaped, female flowers grow as a hairy, yellowish tuft in center of crown; leaves are up to 6.5 feet (2 m) long, pinnate, stiff fronds with pointed leaflets, dark green, leathery
Location: Bright to partly shady, no direct sun; warm, in summer also outdoors if sheltered from rain; in winter, cooler, at 59–64°F (15–18°C)
Care: Keep moderately damp in summer, in winter water less in cool location; mist often; in summer supply with organic fertilizer weekly; propagate from seed (very difficult)
Use: Decorative large plant for use as solitary specimen
Note: All parts of the plant are poisonous.

Growth form:
Herbaceous perennial
Flowering period:
Summer

Cyperus involucratus

Umbrella Plant ✿

Family: Sedge (*Cyperaceae*)
Origin: Damp regions of the tropics and subtropics
Appearance: Grows upright with stiff stalks; wiglike leaf tufts on three-edged stalks, up to 3 feet (1 m) tall; clusters of brown flowers appear in center of tufts
Location: All year round, bright to sunny; also outdoors in summer; tolerates high temperatures in summer with sufficient humidity; can be in somewhat cooler place in winter
Care: Best in a bowl with water; in high temperatures, the soil can also be covered with water; in cool location in winter, keep only damp and mist generously; in summer feed lightly every two weeks, in winter, every four to six weeks if in bright, warm place; propagate by division or by cutting off leaf tuft and rooting it upside down in a glass of water
Use: Popular, low-maintenance, dainty-looking foliage plant for house or conservatory

Growth form:
Herbaceous perennial

D

Dieffenbachia Species and Hybrids

Dumb Cane

Family: Arum lily (*Araceae*)
Origin: Tropical forests of Central/South America, cultivars
Appearance: Herbaceous perennial; short trunklets with stalked leaves; leaves are broad-ovate, large; dark green with highly varied markings in light-green, yellow to creamy white colors
Location: Bright to partly shady, no direct sun; variegated leaves turn green in overly dark location; warm and humid all year round; avoid drafts and temperature fluctuations
Care: Keep evenly and well dampened, avoid waterlogging; mist often; in summer, feed every two weeks, in winter, every four; cut back bare-looking plants in spring
Use: Young plants pretty on windowsill; older ones in conservatory or flower window
Note: The plant may irritate skin and mucous membranes.
Cultivars/Relatives: Many unnamed cultivars are available commercially. Hybrids (→ photo) are common.

Growth form:
Tree, shrub

Dracaena fragrans

Corn Plant ✿

Other names: Fragrant dracaena
Family: Dragon tree (*Dracaenaceae*)
Origin: Tropics and subtropics of Africa, Canary Islands
Appearance: Grows as tree or shrub; dense leaf tufts on more or less long, slender to thick trunks; leaves are lanceolate, narrow or broader, depending on cultivar, solid green, striped, or mottled
Location: All year round, bright but no full sun; warm and as humid as possible, even in winter not below 64°F (18°C); no drafts or low soil temperature
Care: Keep evenly damp all year round, but avoid waterlogging; mist often; in summer, feed every two weeks, in winter, every four to six; occasionally rinse off; sensitive to leaf-shine sprays
Use: Attractive, majestic, and dominant foliage plant, best for offices
Cultivars/Relatives: So-called ti plants, specimens made from sawed-off trunks with lots of leaf tufts, are popular.

Growth form:
Tree, shrub

D

Dracaena marginata

Red-edged Dracaena ✿

Family: Dragon tree (*Dracaenaceae*)
Origin: Tropics and subtropics of Africa, Canary Islands
Appearance: Grows as tree or shrub; one or more leaf tufts on long, sometimes branching trunks; leaves are long, narrow, with red-brown margins
Location: All year round, bright but no full sun; warm and as humid as possible, even in winter not below 64°F (18°C); no drafts or low soil temperatures
Care: Keep evenly damp all year round but avoid waterlogging; mist often; in summer, feed every two weeks, in winter, every four to six weeks; rinse off occasionally; sensitive to leaf-shine sprays
Use: Dainty yet majestic ornamental foliage plant with palm-like flair
Cultivars/Relatives: 'Tricolor' has intense leaf coloration; *D. sanderiana* stays slender and low; *D. surculosa* has broad, spotted leaves; *D. reflexa* 'Song of India' has broad leaf tufts striped with yellow-green.

Growth form:
Climbing plant

Epipremnum pinnatum
Centipede Tongavine

Origin: Tropical forests of the Pacific Islands

Appearance: Has branching stems many meters long, on which clearly stalked leaves are borne; leaves are cordate, leathery, depending on cultivar, dark green with whitish or yellow marking; only the young plant is cultivated, in older plants the leaves are larger

Location: All year round, bright to partly shady, no blazing sun; in overly dark place variegated leaves turn green and spaces between leaves increase; warm all year round

Care: In summer, keep evenly damp, but no waterlogging, drier in winter; in summer, feed every two weeks, in winter, every four weeks; can be cut back hard; propagate from tip and stem cuttings

Use: Fast-growing climbing plant, either in hanging planters or trained to climb a moss pole or trellis

Cultivars/Relatives: *E. aureum* with yellow variegated foliage is also listed as cultivar 'Aureum.'

Growth form: *Tree*
Flowering period: *Early summer*

Eugenia Species

Eugenia Species

Other names: Cherry of the Rio Grande, pitanga, Surinam cherry
Family: Myrtle (*Myrtaceae*)
Origin: Tropical forests of Brazil
Appearance: Slow-growing evergreen trees or shrubs, often sold as bonsai; leaves are small, glossy dark green, reddish during flush; white, brushlike flowers in early summer, turning into cherrylike fruit; in *E. uniflora* (→ photo), the Surinam cherry or pitanga, the fruit is red and tasty
Location: Sunny; outdoors in summer; in winter at 59°F (15°C)
Care: In summer, keep slightly damp and feed every two weeks, water little in winter; tolerates cutting, can also be easily trained as standard
Use: Young or as bonsai for bright rooms, larger plants in containers, also good in conservatory
Note: *E. myriophylla* is also assigned to the botanical genus *Myrciaria*.

Growth form: *Shrub*

x *Fatshedera lizei*

Bush Ivy

Family: Aralia or ivy (*Araliaceae*)

Origin: Bigeneric cross between *Fatsia japonica* and *Hedera hibernica*

Appearance: Bushy and upright, can grow several meters tall, fast-growing; leaves are evergreen, large, with three to five lobes, dark green and glossy; the foliage of the cultivar 'Variegata' is white-variegated (→ photo, right)

Location: Bright to partly shady, 'Variegata' not too dark or leaves will turn green; in summer, normal room temperature, in winter, cooler, at 50–59°F (10–15°C); outdoors in summer, in a spot sheltered from wind and rain

Care: Keep evenly damp in summer, water less in cool location in winter; mist often; in summer, feed every two weeks, in winter, every four weeks; keep pruning to promote bushy growth; propagate from tip cuttings at soil temperature of 68–77°F (20–25°C), or by air layering

Use: Attractive large plant, also suitable for conservatory

Growth form:
Shrub

F

Fatsia japonica

Japanese Aralia

Family: Aralia or ivy (*Araliaceae*)
Origin: Forests of Japan, Ryukyu Islands, South Korea
Appearance: Shrubby, can grow several meters tall; leaves are evergreen, seven- to nine-lobed long stalks, to 15 inches (40 cm) wide, dark green, glossy; white-variegated cultivars are also available commercially
Location: Bright to shady; cool in summer, in winter at 43–54°F (6–12°C); cultivars with colored foliage not too dark and in winter not below 59°F (15°C); in summer best outdoors in sheltered spot, avoid direct sun
Care: In summer, keep evenly and well dampened, but no waterlogging; in winter, keep drier; mist often, especially in warmer location; in summer, feed lightly every two to three weeks, in winter, every six weeks; propagate from seed or tip cuttings or by air layering
Use: Good for stairwells or anterooms; also as container plant for conservatory, balcony, and patio
Note: All parts of the plant contain toxins.

Growth form:
Tree, shrub

Ficus benjamina

Weeping Fig

Family: Mulberry (*Moraceae*)
Origin: Southeast Asia to southwestern Pacific
Appearance: Usually tree or bush; leaves are evergreen, dark green, usually glossy, broad-oval with pointed tip, in cultivars also with white or cream-colored patterns, some with wavy margins
Location: All year round, bright but no full sun; warm in summer, cooler in winter
Care: Water moderately in summer, keep drier in winter if in cool place; mist often, especially in winter if in warm place; in summer, feed lightly every two weeks, in winter, every four weeks; propagate by air layering
Use: For living spaces, hallway, office, conservatory; large specimens are especially attractive
Note: Leaf drop increases with drafts, temperature fluctuations, and sharp alternation between damp and dry. It is often grown as a standard and can be found with decoratively interwoven trunks.

Growth
form:
Tree

Ficus elastica / F. lyrata

Rubber Plant/Fiddle-Leaf Fig ✿

Other Names: *F. elastica* also known as rubber fig
Family: Mulberry (*Moraceae*)
Origin: *F. elastica,* eastern Himalayas to Malay Archipelago,
F. lyrata (→ photo), tropics of Africa
Appearance: Grows as tree; leaves are evergreen, dark green,
very large, in rubber plant broad-oval, leathery, in fiddle-leaf
fig shaped like a fiddle and matte; in cultivars also variegated
Location: All year round, bright, no full sun; warm in
summer, cooler in winter
Care: Water moderately in summer, in winter keep drier in
cool location; mist often, especially in winter if in warm
location; in summer, feed lightly every two weeks, in winter,
every four weeks; propagate by air layering
Use: Older specimens especially good-looking in living
spaces, hallway, office, conservatory
Cultivars/Relatives: *F. rubiginosa* (rusty fig) and
F. macrocarpa resemble the rubber plant.

Growth form: *Climbing shrub*

Ficus pumila

Creeping Fig

Other names: Climbing fig
Family: Mulberry (*Moraceae*)
Origin: China, Vietnam, Japan
Appearance: Thin-stemmed, growth habit prostrate, hanging, or also climbing (holds on with suckers); leaves are evergreen, ovate, thin; in cultivars also white-variegated
Location: All year round, bright, no full sun; warm in summer, in winter at room temperature or cooler, not below 41°F (5°C)
Care: In summer, water moderately, in winter keep drier if in cool location; mist often, especially in warm location in winter; in summer, feed lightly every two weeks, in winter, every four weeks; prune in late winter to stimulate bushy growth
Use: Charming foliage plant for many occasions, very pretty in hanging planters
Cultivars/Relatives: 'Serpyllifolium' has especially small leaves; *F. sagittata* is a climber with pointed leaves.

Growth form: *Herbaceous perennial*

Fittonia Species

Fittonia

Other names: Mosaic plant

Family: Acanthus (*Acanthaceae*)

Origin: Tropical forests from Columbia to Bolivia

Appearance: *F. gigantea* grows upright to 24 inches (60 cm) high, *F. verschaffeltii* is creeping, with stems that root upon ground contact; leaves are ovate, striking mosaic-like veining, in *F. gigantea* dark green with red marking, in *F. verschaffeltii* (→ photo) white, silvery, or reddish-veined, depending on cultivar

Location: Partly shady to shady; warm all year round, even in winter not below 64°F (18°C); humid air, avoid drafts

Care: Keep moderately damp, no waterlogging, mist often; in summer, feed every two weeks, in winter, every four weeks; propagate from tip cuttings at soil temperature of about 68°F (20°C)

Use: For cramped places, ground cover in warm conservatory or greenhouse, flower windows, mini-greenhouses, hanging planters, and bowls

Cultivars/Relatives: *F. verschaffeltii* 'Minima' is often planted in bottle gardens.

Growth form:
Subshrub

Gynura Species

Gynura

Other names: Velvet plant
Family: Aster, daisy, or sunflower (*Asteraceae*)
Origin: Tropical regions of Africa and Asia
Appearance: Semishrubs, also producing long stems for climbing; leaves are oblong, with toothed margins, dark green, thickly covered with violet to purple hairs
Location: All year round, very bright but no direct sun; room temperature, in winter also slightly cooler but not below 64°F (18°C); humid air; dark location makes leaves turn green
Care: Keep slightly damp; high humidity, don't mist leaves directly; in summer feed lightly every week, in winter, every three to four weeks; prune regularly; plants attractive only when young, replace with new ones after two years; propagate from tip cuttings
Use: Striking color effect, best in hanging planters
Note: All parts of the plant are toxic.
Cultivars/Relatives: *G. aurantiaca* 'Purple Passion' (→ photo) and *G. procumbens* are widely available.

H

Growth form:
Climbing shrub

Hedera Species

Ivy

Family: Aralia or ivy (*Araliaceae*)

Origin: Forests of Europe, Asia, North Africa, and North America

Appearance: Climbing shrubs; some are trained as standards or on wire frames or shaped; leaves are evergreen, three- to five-lobed, changing shape as they age, only the young form is sold as a house plant; depending on species and cultivar, large- or small-leaved, heavily or slightly lobed, pure green or flecked with white, yellow, silver, or several colors

Location: Bright to shady, no full sun; moderately warm, cooler in winter; variegated and large-leafed cultivars brighter and warmer in general; in summer also outdoors

Care: Keep evenly damp, water less in winter; in summer, feed every two weeks, in winter, every four weeks; prune in spring; propagate from tip or stem cuttings

Use: For hanging planters, climbing frames, stairwells

Note: The fruit is highly poisonous.

Growth form:
Palm

Howea Species

Kentia Palm ✿

Other names: Thatch palm, sentry palm
Family: Palm (*Arecaceae*, *Palmae*)
Origin: Lord Howe Islands in the Pacific
Appearance: Single-trunked, but usually planted in groups for more luxuriant effect; in *H. belmoreana* the fronds are erect and droop slightly, in *H. forsteriana* the leaves are splayed; leaves are long, evenly pinnate fronds; dark green, in *H. forsteriana* (→ photo) dotted beneath
Location: All year round, bright to partly shady, no blazing sun; warm and airy, even in winter not below 64°F (18°C); older plants also outdoors in summer, in protected spot
Care: Keep evenly and slightly damp, but no waterlogging, in winter, water less if in cooler location, but don't let substrate dry out; in summer, feed lightly every two weeks, in winter, every four to six weeks, mist frequently
Use: Decorative palm for indoor use and conservatories, also outdoors as container plant in summer

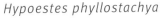

Growth form:
Shrub

Hypoestes phyllostachya

Polka-Dot Plant

Other names: Freckle-face plant
Family: Acanthus (*Acanthaceae*)
Origin: Tropical forests of Madagascar
Appearance: Small, densely branching shrub, tends to be herbaceous in cultivation; leaves are 2–4 inches (5–10 cm) long, entire-margined, ovate, olive-green to dark green, depending on cultivar, with striking red, pink, or white dots
Location: All year round, very bright, no direct sun, leaves turn green in dark location; warm and humid
Care: All year round, keep moderately damp and mist generously with lime-poor water; in summer, feed every two weeks, in winter every four; usually grown only for a year, as plants quickly grow leggy and leaf coloration fades, so don't delay propagation; regular pruning of young plants promotes bushy growth; propagate from seed or tip cuttings
Use: Colorful foliage plant that needs little space; also good as ground cover or underplanting

Growth form: *Herbaceous perennial*
Flowering period: *Summer*

Isolepis cernua

Slender Clubrush

Other names: Fiber-optic grass; previously named *Scirpus cernuus*
Family: Sedge (*Cyperaceae*)
Origin: Mediterranean region, South and East Africa, Australia, New Zealand
Appearance: Grows clumplike with upright to slightly overhanging culms bearing small, brownish flowers at the tips; leaves are long, thin, rushlike culms, fresh green
Location: All year round, bright to partly shady, no blazing sun, warm, can also be in cooler spot in winter but not below 54°F (12°C); air as humid as possible
Care: Keep well dampened, if in warm place also tolerates wet feet; if overwintered in cool place, drier, but don't allow to dry out; keep humidity high; in summer, feed every two weeks, in winter, every six weeks
Use: Hanging planters or atop columns; suitable for water or swamp gardens, but should not be completely in water
Note: The plant does not tolerate chemical insecticides.

Growth form:
Tree
Flowering period:
March–Apr.

Jacaranda mimosifolia

Blue Jacaranda

Family: Trumpet creeper (*Bignoniaceae*)
Origin: South America, predominantly Argentina
Appearance: In native habitat, large trees, but markedly smaller when grown in pots; in native habitat, striking blue flowers appear before leaf flush, in pot culture only large plants flower; leaves are long, pinnate, resembling mimosa or ferns, dark green
Location: All year round, very bright; warm in summer, somewhat cooler in winter but not below 57°F (14°C)
Care: In summer, keep evenly and slightly damp, in winter water little if in cool place, but don't let root ball dry out; mist often; in summer, feed every two to three weeks, in winter, not at all; usually loses all leaves in winter, but new growth appears in spring; propagate from seed at 68–77°F (20–25°C), soften seed in water 24 hours in advance
Use: Young plants indoors, older ones as container plants in conservatory

Growth form:
Palm

Latania lontaroides

Red Latan Palm

Family: Palm (*Arecaceae, Palmae*)

Origin: Mauritius and the Mascarenes

Appearance: Grows upright; gray-green leaves form a thick tuft, like large fans on long, faintly reddish stalks

Location: All year round, bright to partly shady, does not tolerate direct sun; evenly warm, temperature not below 64°F (18°C) in winter and at night; humidity as high as possible

Care: Keep damp all year round, placing pot in water-filled saucer; in winter, water slightly less if in cooler place, never allow to dry out; keep humidity high; in summer, feed every two weeks, in winter, every four weeks; propagate from seed

Use: Elegant, but somewhat fussy and high-maintenance exotic beauty, ideal in warm conservatory

Cultivars/Relatives: Occasionally *L. loddigesii* and *L. verschaffeltii* are available commercially.

Growth form:
Palm

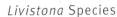

Livistona Species

Livistona

Family: Palms (*Arecaceae, Palmae*)
Origin: Japan, Taiwan, islands of Southeast Asia to Australia
Appearance: Leaves borne in thick tufts, usually stiffly erect with arching ends; even when young, there are large, deeply divided fans on toothed leafstalks, glossy dark green
Location: Year round, as bright as possible to sunny, in summer also outdoors in a sheltered spot; warm and airy, cooler in winter at 59°F (15°C)
Care: Keep evenly damp in growing season, in winter water little if in cool place, but don't let root ball dry out; in summer, feed every two weeks, in winter, every four to six weeks; mist frequently
Use: Attractive for large rooms and conservatories
Note: The sharp-toothed leafstalks can cause injuries.
Cultivars/Relatives: *L. australis, L. chinensis* (→ photo, needs less light), and *L. rotundifolia* are commercially available.

Growth form:
Palm

Lytocaryum weddelianum
Wedding Palm

Other names: Previously known as *Microcoelum weddelianum*
Family: Palm (*Arecaceae, Palmae*)
Origin: Tropical rain forests of Brazil
Appearance: Upright, with leaves borne on a slender trunk and slightly drooping; usually several are planted together; dainty fronds with narrow leaflets, light green on top, gray-green beneath, stalks and midrib covered with black-red scales
Location: Bright all year round, no direct sun; warm, even in winter and at night not below 68°F (20°C); does not tolerate drafts or low soil temperature; humidity as high as possible
Care: Keep evenly damp all year round, but avoid waterlogging at all costs; keep humidity high; in summer, feed every two weeks, in winter, every four to six weeks; propagate from seed at soil temperature of 86°F (30°C)
Use: Pretty ornamental plant for enclosed flower window, mini-greenhouse, or warm conservatory

Growth form:
Herbaceous perennial

M

Maranta leuconeura

Prayer Plant

Other names: Ten Commandments
Family: Prayer plant (*Marantaceae*)
Origin: Tropical rain forests of Brazil
Appearance: Herbaceous with tuberous roots from which the long-stalked leaves arise; leaves are large, oval, depending on cultivar, light or emerald green with red or pink veins; young leaves are rolled; at night, the leaves fold upward
Location: Bright to partly shady, but no direct sun; warm and humid all year round; protect from drafts; does not tolerate low soil temperature
Care: Demanding in regard to water supply; keep evenly damp, use lime-poor water; keep humidity high, but don't spray directly; in summer, feed lightly every two weeks, in winter, every four weeks; propagate by division or from tip cuttings
Use: Eye-catching plant for warm rooms

Growth form: *Climbing shrub*

Monstera deliciosa

Split-Leaf Philodendron ❀

Family: Arum lily (*Araceae*)
Origin: Tropical forests of Mexico
Appearance: Climbing plant several meters high; sends long aerial roots downward, where they root upon contact with soil; leaves are large, leathery, first green and entire-margined, later dark green with holes or slits, some cultivars are variegated
Location: All year round, bright, no direct sun, and warm; can also be in cooler spot in winter; at temperatures below 59°F (15°C) and in overly dark place, growth virtually ceases
Care: Keep evenly and slightly damp, but avoid waterlogging; mist often; in summer, feed every two weeks, in winter, every four weeks; don't cut off aerial roots; propagate from tip cuttings or by air layering
Use: Imposing, very long-lived large plant; needs climbing support
Note: The plant contains skin irritants. Club-shaped inflorescence with involucral leaf may appear on older plants.

Growth form:
Shrub

Muehlenbeckia complexa

Maidenhair Vine

Other names: Mattress vine, wire vine
Family: Knotweed (*Polygonaceaea*)
Origin: Rocky regions and forests of New Zealand
Appearance: Small shrub with thin, meter-long stems
with which it creeps over the ground or climbs up a support;
'Nana' stays smaller and does not wind; small, rounded leaves,
light green to fresh green
Location: Bright to partly shady, no blazing midday sun;
fairly cool and airy all year round
Care: Keep evenly and slightly damp; in summer, feed every
two weeks, in winter, every four weeks; cut into any shape;
propagate by division or from cuttings at 68–77°F (20–25°C)
Use: For cool rooms or conservatories; often trained
around wire arches or other climbing aids; also suitable
for hanging planters
Cultivars/Relatives: *M. axillaris,* with a creeping growth
habit, is similar; in winter it tolerates temperatures down
to 41°F (5°C).

Growth form:
Shrub
Flowering period:
June–Oct.

Myrtus communis

True Myrtle

Family: Myrtle (*Myrtaceae*)
Origin: Around the Mediterranean, Asia Minor to Iran
Appearance: Shrubby growth, in cultivation 3–5 feet
(1–1.5 m) tall, otherwise taller; in summer small
white flowers appear, developing into black berries; leaves
are evergreen, small, oblong and pointed, dark green, leathery
Location: In summer, sunny and warm, outdoors if possible;
in winter, bright, at 41–50°F (5–10°C)
Care: In summer, keep slightly damp with lime-poor water,
in winter, water just enough to keep root ball from drying
out; until August feed every two weeks, in winter not at all;
very tolerant of cutting, can be trained into pyramids or tiny
trees with crowns; propagate from semilignified tip cuttings
in late spring
Use: In conservatory or as container plant
Note: The plant has a long tradition for medicinal uses.
The leaves are aromatic when touched.

Growth form: *Herbaceous perennial*

Nephrolepis exaltata

Boston Fern

Other names: Sword fern
Family: Sword fern (*Nephrolepidaceae*)
Origin: Tropical forests worldwide
Appearance: Forms thick clumps with erect to pendent fronds, depending on cultivar, large and wide-spreading or dainty and more compact; rhizomes produce many offsets; leaves are long, sword-shaped fronds with sickle-shaped pinnae, light green; various cultivars, some very old, with wavy, curly, twisted, or bipinnate fronds, also with yellow-green coloring
Location: All year round, bright to partly shady; warm, even in winter not below 64°F (18°C); air as humid as possible
Care: Keep evenly and slightly damp but avoid waterlogging, in winter drier if in cool spot; mist often; in summer, feed weekly; propagate from offsets, by division, or from spores
Use: Attractive as hanging plant or atop a column
Cultivars/Relatives: *N. cordifolia* has narrower fronds.

Growth form: *Herbaceous perennial*
Flowering period: *March–Oct.*

Pachystachys lutea

Golden Shrimp Plant

Other names: Lollipop plant
Family: Acanthus (*Acanthaceae*)
Origin: Tropical forests of South America
Appearance: Herbaceous shrub; at ends of stems are long-lasting, candlelike spikes of bright yellow bracts like overlapping scales, surrounding inconspicuous white, very short-lived flowers; leaves are about 4 inches (10 cm) long, oblong-oval, dark green, and slightly wrinkled
Location: All year round, very bright, in summer protect from blazing midday sun; warm, even in winter above 64–68°F (18–20°C); humidity as high as possible; no cold feet.
Care: Keep slightly damp all year round; mist often; in summer, feed every two weeks, in winter, every four to six weeks; usually treated with growth retardants, whose effect rapidly decreases; propagate from tip cuttings at 77°F (25°C)
Use: Brilliant splash of color, has effect of ornamental flowering plant
Cultivars/Relatives: *P. coccinea* has green bracts and red flowers.

Growth form: *Herbaceous perennial*

Pellaea Species
Cliff Brake Fern

Family: Maidenhair fern (*Adiantaceae*)
Origin: America, New Zealand, Africa, Mascarenes, Sri Lanka
Appearance: Grows in clumps with pendant fronds arising from short rhizomes; *P. rotundifolia* (button fern, → photo) and *P. atropurpurea* are small and dainty, *P. viridis* grows slightly larger. Most commonly available is *P. rotundifolia*, with small, rounded, leathery pinnae, dark green with often reddish midrib; *P. atropurpurea* has red-brown, sometimes bipinnate fronds; *P. viridis* has dark-green, bi- to tripinnate fronds on blackish stalks
Location: Bright to partly shady, also sunny, no blazing midday sun, in summer outdoors in protected spot; all year round at room temperature, in winter also somewhat cooler
Care: In summer, keep slightly damp, drier in winter; in summer, feed lightly every two weeks; propagate by division or from spores
Use: Pretty in hanging planters

Growth form:
Herbaceous perennial
Flowering period:
All year round

Peperomia obtusifolia

Baby Rubber Plant ✿

Other names: Peperomia
Family: Pepper (*Piperaceae*)
Origin: Tropical and subtropical America
Appearance: Herbaceous, bushy, with upright stems; leaves are evergreen, elliptical, leathery, dull green; inflorescences like mouse tails appear all year round
Location: Bright to partly shady, also in winter, but no direct sun; warm all year round, even in winter not below 64°F (18°C); humidity as high as possible
Care: Keep slightly damp all year round, but not wet, mist tender-leaved cultivars often; in summer, feed every two weeks, in winter, only once a month; propagate from tip, stem, or leaf cuttings
Use: Low-maintenance foliage plant for house, conservatory, flower window, and mini-greenhouse
Cultivars/Relatives: *P. caperata* (emerald ripple peperomia) has wrinkled, cordate leaves; this species also has cultivars with variegated leaves.

Growth form:
Herbaceous perennial
Flowering period:
All year round

P

Peperomia rotundifolia

Creeping Peperomia ✿

Other names: Peperomia, yerba Linda
Family: Pepper (*Piperaceae*)
Origin: Southeastern Brazil
Appearance: Herbaceous, procumbent or pendant; leaves are evergreen, rounded, fleshy, light green; inflorescences like mouse tails appear all year round
Location: Bright to partly shady, also in winter, but no direct sun; warm all year round, even in winter not below 64°F (18°C); also tolerates dry air
Care: All year round, keep slightly damp but not wet; appreciates occasional misting; in summer, feed every two weeks, in winter, only once a month; best to cut back in spring, if needed; propagate from tip, stem, or leaf cuttings
Use: Easy-care foliage plant, also pretty in hanging planters or atop columns
Cultivars/Relatives: *P. scandens* and *P. glabella* also are pendulous; they are usually available in variegated forms.

Growth form:
Shrub

Philodendron bipinnatifidum

Cut-Leaf Philodendron

Other names: Tree philodendron; also listed as *P. selloum*
Family: Arum lily (*Araceae*)
Origin: Tropical rain forests of the Americas
Appearance: Upright shrub, usually with aerial roots; leaves deeply cut to slit, rich green, glossy, to 3 feet (1 m) long
Location: All year round, bright to partly shady, avoid direct sun; warm location, in winter cooler at night but not below 60°F (16°C)
Care: Keep evenly and slightly damp, mist often; in summer, feed every two weeks, in winter every four to six weeks; can be cut back, but don't remove aerial roots; propagate from tip or stem cuttings, air layering also possible
Use: Robust, for house, office, conservatory
Cultivars/Relatives: *P. martianum* has lanceolate, dark green leaves with inflated leaf stalks; *P. melanochrysum* bears heart-shaped to arrow-shaped leaves.

Growth form:
Climbing shrub

Philodendron scandens

Heart-Leaf Philodendron ✤

Other names: Parlor ivy, sweetheart vine
Family: Arum lily (*Araceae*)
Origin: Tropical rain forests of the Americas
Appearance: Climbing or pendent shrub; leaves are cordate, glossy dark green, growing larger with age; occasionally with aerial roots
Location: All year round, bright to partly shady, avoid direct sun; warm location, in winter cooler at night but not below 60°F (16°C)
Care: Keep evenly and slightly damp, mist often; in summer, feed every two weeks, in winter, every four to six weeks; can be cut back but never remove aerial roots; propagate from tip cuttings
Use: In hanging planters or atop columns, also climbing on moss pole; always dapper, easy-care foliage plant for house, office, conservatory
Note: All parts of the plant contain skin irritants and allergens.

Growth form:
Palm

Phoenix Species

Date Palm

Family: Palm (*Arecaceae, Palmae*)
Origin: Canary Islands, Africa, and western, southern to southeastern Asia
Appearance: *P. canariensis:* spiky to arching fronds on a thick, fairly short trunk; *P. roebelenii:* arching fronds on low, slender trunk, often multitrunked; leaves are large fronds, in *P. canariensis*, the Canary Island date palm, leathery and dark green, in *P. roebelenii* (→ photo), the pygmy date palm, leathery and dark green, soft
Location: Sunny all year round, in summer best outdoors, except for *P. roebelenii*; warm, in winter also at 50°F (10°C), *P. roebelenii* not below 64°F (18°C)
Care: Keep evenly and slightly damp, drier in winter if in cool place; mist *P. roebelenii* often or leaf tips will turn brown; in summer, feed every two weeks, in winter not at all; propagate from seed
Use: For house and conservatory; also as container plants; *P. roebelenii* best in flower window

Growth form:
Herbaceous perennial

P

Pilea Species

Clearweed

Family: Nettle (*Urticaceae*)
Origin: Tropical and subtropical forests
Appearance: Low, herbaceous plants, annual or perennial; leaves are variable, many with striking markings, several cultivars not easily assignable to a species; *P. cardierei* (→ photo): broad-lanceolate, medium-green leaves with silvery, slightly raised spots; *P. involucrata:* rounded-oval, dark green leaves, reddish beneath with hairy, puckered surface, often with lighter margin; *P. microphylla:* small, rounded, light green leaves
Location: All year round, bright to partly shady; warm, *P. cardierei* and *P. microphylla* not below 50°F (10°C) in winter
Care: Keep evenly and slightly damp, in winter water little if in cool place; in summer, feed every two weeks, in winter, every four to six weeks; mist often
Use: Charming, doesn't take up much room
Note: Ripe stamens release pollen in puffs when touched.

Growth form:
Climbing shrub

Piper Species

Pepper

Family: Pepper (*Piperaceae*)
Origin: Tropical regions of the world
Appearance: Perennial climbers that need help to climb;
P. ornatum (→ photo) bears long-stalked, broad, cordate,
dark green, waxy leaves with white marking; *P. crocatum*
(also listed as *P. ornatum* 'Crocatum') has cordate, long,
pointed, dark green leaves with pink to whitish veining
Location: Bright to partly shady, no direct sun; warm all year
round, even in winter not below 64°F (18°C); needs high
humidity; protect from drafts and "cold feet"
Care: Keep evenly and slightly damp and ensure high
humidity; in summer, feed every one to two weeks,
in winter, every four to six; propagate from stem cuttings
Use: Decorative in hanging planter or as climber,
best in enclosed flower window, mini-greenhouse,
or warm conservatory

Growth form:
Shrub
Flowering period:
Spring, summer

Pisonia umbellifera 'Variegata'

Map Plant

Other names: Bird-catcher plant
Family: Four O'Clock (*Nyctaginaceae*)
Origin: New Zealand, Australia, Mauritius, Norfolk Islands
Appearance: Large shrub or small tree, but markedly lower when grown indoors; in natural habitat with flowers and fruit that exude a sticky substance to which insects and small birds stick, hence the name; leaves are elliptical to lanceolate, to 15 inches (40 cm) long, decussate, thin, leathery, glossy; dark green with light green and creamy white markings; the true species is dark green
Location: Very bright, but no direct sun; warm all year round, high soil temperature especially in winter
Care: Always keep slightly damp; mist often and rinse off occasionally; in summer, feed every one to two weeks, in winter, every four to six on average; propagate from tip cuttings at soil temperature of 77°F (25°C) or by air layering
Use: Effective as ornamental foliage plant

Growth form: *Herbaceous perennial*

Platycerium bifurcatum

Staghorn Fern

Family: Common fern (*Polypodiaceae*)
Origin: Forests of New Guinea and Australia
Appearance: Epiphytic; fronds are obliquely upright, lobes pendulous; two kinds of fronds: sterile clasping fronds also absorb water and nutrients, they overlap and die eventually; large, leathery, dark green, antler-shaped fronds produce spores and have felt-like coating
Location: All year round, bright to partly shady, no direct sun; warm, in winter above 59°F (15°C); humid air
Care: Pour decalcified water into nest-like sterile fronds or immerse weekly; in summer, feed very lightly every three to four weeks; ensure high humidity but do not mist; use orchid substrate
Use: For hanging planters, epiphyte logs, orchid baskets, enclosed flower windows or mini-greenhouses
Cultivars/Relatives: Various cultivars are commercially available.

Growth form:
Herbaceous perennial

Plectranthus Species

Swedish Ivy

Family: Mint (*Lamiaceae*)

Origin: Tropics and subtropics of the world, except the Americas

Appearance: Bushy, with long, pendulous or procumbent stems; leaves are ovate, with serrate or toothed margin; exuding an intense scent when rubbed; *P. forsteri* 'Marginatus' (→ photo): previously *P. coleoides* 'Marginatus,' variegated Swedish ivy, light green leaves with broad white margin; *P. oertendahlii*: small, more rounded, light to medium green, white-veined leaves

Location: Very bright to sunny and airy, in summer also outdoors; warm, in winter not below 59°F (15°C)

Care: Keep evenly damp in summer, drier in winter if in cool place; in summer, feed weekly, in winter, every four weeks; propagate from tip cuttings, prune young plants frequently

Use: Hanging plant for planters and bowls, balcony and patio, or as ground cover in conservatory; *P. oertendahlii* also in bottle gardens

Growth form: *Herbaceous perennial*

Pogonatherum paniceum

Baby Bamboo ✿

Family: Grass (*Poaceae*)

Origin: Grasslands of China, Malaysia, and Australia

Appearance: Low-growing, depending on cultivar to 24 inches (60 cm) tall, clumplike, culms are crowded, erect at first, then pendulous and heavily branched in upper part; leaves are evergreen, short, narrow, on thin but strong stalks; fresh green; there are also various cultivars, some with yellow-variegated leaves

Location: All year round, sunny to bright, in summer also outdoors; warm, but can be cooler in winter at maximum of 60°F (16°C)

Care: Water generously all year round, also tolerates "foot baths" in summer, in winter don't allow to dry out, even in cool location; in summer, feed every two weeks, in winter, every six weeks; propagate by division or from root offsets

Use: Pretty house plant; cats are fond of nibbling at this grass and can be offered this instead of "real" cat grass

Growth form:
Shrub

Polyscias Species

Ming Aralia

Family: Aralia or ivy (*Araliaceae*)
Origin: Tropical forests of Asia and Polynesia
Appearance: Small trees or shrubs; most common is
P. scutellaria 'Balfour' (previously *P. balfouriana*), whose
heart- to kidney-shaped leaves are medium green with
white margins and spots; *P. filicifolia* (→ photo) has frond-
like, deeply cut, light green leaves; *P. guilfoylei* and *P. fruticosa*
have pinnate leaves, depending on cultivar, white-variegated
Location: Bright to partly shady, no direct sun; all year round,
warm, also at night not below 64°F (18°C); humidity as high
as possible
Care: Always keep moderately damp, but avoid waterlogging;
mist often, both with lime-poor water; in summer, feed every
two weeks, in winter, every four weeks
Use: Graceful ornamental foliage plant, but high-maintenance;
especially attractive as small trees in bonsai fashion

Growth form: *Herbaceous perennial*

Polystichum tsus-simense

Tsus-Sima Holly Fern

Other names: Korean rock fern
Family: Wood fern (*Dryopteridaceae*)
Origin: Forests of Japan, China, Korea, Taiwan
Appearance: Forms low rosettes like shuttlecocks; fronds are upright at first, later pendulous; leaves are small, pinnate fronds, the individual leaflets are leathery, serrate, and end in a sharp point; dark green; petioles covered with dark-brown scales
Location: All year round, bright to partly shady, in summer also outdoors in a protected spot; not too warm, in winter also cool, not below 41°F (5°C)
Care: In summer, keep evenly damp, in winter, water less if in cool place; in summer, feed lightly every two to three weeks; propagate by division or from seed
Use: Pretty fern for indoors or cold conservatory, also suitable for bottle gardens
Cultivars/Relatives: *P. auriculatum* for greenhouse or enclosed flower window is occasionally available.

Growth form:
Shrub
Flowering period:
June–Sept.

Pseuderanthemum atropurpureum

Purple False Eranthemum

Family: Acanthus (*Acanthaceae*)
Origin: Tropical forests of Polynesia
Appearance: Shrubby; evergreen; leaves are ovate to broad-elliptical, pointed, dark green; sometimes also with metallic sheen, with white, yellowish, light green, pink, or purple spots
Location: Bright to partly shady, does not tolerate sun; all year round, warm, even in winter not below 64°F (18°C), high soil temperature; humid air
Care: Keep evenly and slightly damp, but avoid waterlogging and mist often, both with lime-poor water; in summer, feed lightly every two weeks, in winter, every four to six weeks; propagate from semi-lignified cuttings at soil temperature of 59°F (15°C); frequent pruning stimulates branching
Use: Colorful ornamental foliage plant, good grouped with green plants
Cultivars/Relatives: 'Tricolor' has purple, creamy yellow, and pink patterns on leaves.

Growth form: *Herbaceous perennial*

Pteris Species

Brake Fern

Family: Brake (*Pteridaceae*)

Origin: Tropical and subtropical forests, Mediterranean region

Appearance: Dainty, bushy growth, from rhizomes; *P. tremula* larger and fast-growing; leaves are fronds, pinnate or multi-pinnate, some crinkled at tip; most popular is *P. cretica* (→ photo): many cultivars with highly variable, sometimes variegated fronds; *P. ensiformis* in cultivars with white or silvery variegation; *P. argyraea*, dark green with silver middle stripe; *P. tremula* has long, medium-green fronds

Location: Partly shady; warm, in winter to 54°F (12°C); no drafts; colored cultivars brighter and warmer

Care: Water evenly with lime-poor water, keep drier in winter; mist often; in summer, feed very lightly every two weeks

Use: In the house or not overly warm conservatory, *P. argyraea* in enclosed flower window

Growth form: *Tree*

R

Radermachera sinica

China Doll

Family: Trumpet creeper (*Bignoniaceae*)
Origin: Regions in southeastern China
Appearance: Grows as small tree; treated with growth retardants to create bushy look; when their effect decreases the plant can grow to 5–6½ feet (1.5–2 m); leaves are evergreen, bipinnate, dark green, glossy; the various cultivars differ mainly in the size of their leaves
Location: Bright all year round; in summer warm, also outdoors, in winter cooler but not below 54°F (12°C)
Care: Keep moderately damp in summer and mist often, both with lime-poor water; in winter, water only sparingly but don't let root ball dry out; in summer, feed every two to three weeks; propagate from seed (light generator) or from tip cuttings
Use: Very effective ornamental foliage plant, good as solitary specimen
Note: Reacts to heavy cigarette smoke by dropping leaves.

Growth form:
Palm

Rhapis Species

Lady Palm

Other names: Bamboo palm
Family: Palm (*Arecaceae, Palmae*)
Origin: Forest regions in southern China
Appearance: Forms multi-trunked groups; the slender, bamboo-like trunks grow from underground rhizomes; *R. humilis* grows to only 3 feet (1 m), *R. excelsa* somewhat taller and wider; leaves are fingerlike fans, dark green, glossy; in *R. humilis* the individual pinnae are daintier and more numerous than in *R. excelsa* (→ photo)
Location: Bright to partly shady, but no direct sun; in summer also outdoors in a sheltered spot; avoid drafts; not too warm, in winter, cool, 41–50°F (5–10°C)
Care: Water heavily in summer, in winter only enough to keep root ball from drying out completely; in summer feed every two weeks
Use: Dainty palm for indoors, stairwells, or cool conservatory; also trained as bonsai

Growth form:
Climbing shrub

R

Rhoicissus capensis

Evergreen Grape

Other names: Cape grape
Family: Grape (*Vitaceae*)
Origin: Subtropical regions in South Africa
Appearance: Vigorous, fast-growing climbing shrub; has tuberous underground storage organs; leaves are evergreen, large, almost heart-shaped, emarginated, leathery, glossy dark green, with reddish hairs beneath, borne on long stalks
Location: Bright to partly shady, no direct sun; in summer, also in a shady spot outdoors; not too warm, keep cooler in winter, about 50°F (10°C)
Care: In summer, keep evenly damp but avoid waterlogging, drier in winter if in cool place; mist often; in summer, feed every two to three weeks, in winter, every four to six; needs sturdy climbing aid; if need be, cut back in spring
Use: Robust climber for stairwell, hallway, entry area, or cold conservatory

Growth form:
Palm

Sabal Species

Sabal Palm

Other names: Palmetto palm
Family: Palm (*Arecaceae*, *Palmae*)
Origin: Subtropical regions of the U.S.A., Caribbean islands
Appearance: *S. minor* (dwarf palmetto, → photo), a small-growing species, forms a short underground stem barely rising above surface, from which bushy leaf tuft emerges; *S. palmetto* (cabbage palm) bears a thick, compact leaf tuft atop a long, slender stem, strikingly marked by petiole remnants. Leaves are large, deeply cut, long-stalked fans; in *S. minor*, blue-green, in *S. palmetto*, dark green
Location: All year round, very bright, not too sunny; in summer best outdoors; warm, in winter cooler, at 50–59°F (10–15°C)
Care: Water generously in summer, in winter only enough to keep root ball from drying out; mist occasionally; in summer, feed lightly every two weeks
Use: Plant adds subtropical flair indoors and in not-overly-warm conservatories; also good as container plant

Growth form:
Subshrub

Sanchezia parvibracteata

Sanchezia

Family: Acanthus (*Acanthaceae*)
Origin: Tropical rain forests of South America and the Pacific Islands
Appearance: Bushy, slightly branching subshrub; evergreen; leaves are broad-oblong, to 11½ inches (30 cm); dark green with yellowish central rib and veins, 'Variegata' has golden yellow marking
Location: Bright to partly shady, no blazing midday sun, but also not too dark; warm all year round, even in winter not below 60–64°F (16–18°C); as humid as possible
Care: Keep evenly and slightly damp, but avoid waterlogging; ensure high humidity; in summer, feed every two weeks, in winter, every four to six weeks; also tolerates hard cutting back; propagate from tip cuttings
Use: Attractive ornamental foliage plant that does best in enclosed flower window, mini-greenhouse, or warm conservatory

Growth form: *Herbaceous perennial*

Sansevieria trifasciata

Snake Plant ✿

Family: Dragon tree (*Dracaenaceae*)
Origin: Tropical regions in West Africa
Appearance: Very erect, the 'Hahnii' cultivars rosette-like; leaves are evergreen, sword-shaped, to 3 feet (1 m) long, coarse, with dark- or light-green transverse bands; various cultivars: 'Laurentii' with yellow leaf margins, 'Silver Cloud' with silver pattern; 'Hahnii,' greenleaved, 'Golden Hahnii,' yellow striped, 'Silver Hahnii,' with silvery spots
Location: Very bright to sunny, the true species also partly shady; warm, even in winter not below 59°F (15°C)
Care: Water only when soil is dry, in winter even less if in cool place; in summer, apply cactus food monthly; repot annually, as it is fast-growing; propagate by division or from 2-inch (5-cm)-long leaf cuttings
Use: Easy-care plant with nostalgic charm, good for novices
Note: All parts of the plant are poisonous and the leaf tips are very sharp.

Growth form:
Herbaceous perennial
Flowering period:
May–Aug.

Saxifraga stolonifera

Strawberry Begonia

Family: Saxifrage (*Saxifragaceae*)
Origin: Forests of Japan and China
Appearance: Herbaceous perennial with rosettelike habit; numerous stolons develop on long offsets; in summer months, tiny white flowers appear in panicles; leaves are rounded to kidney-shaped, hairy, notched on margin, on long stalks, dark green above with white veins, purple beneath; in 'Tricolor,' leaves are green with broad, white margin and pink tinge
Location: Bright to partly shady, in summer also outdoors; airy and cool, tolerates to 41°F (5°C) in winter, 'Tricolor' not below 59°F (15°C)
Care: Keep moderately damp, in winter somewhat drier if in cool place; in summer, feed every two weeks, in winter, every four to six; propagate from stolons, always put several in a pot
Use: Popular in hanging planters, also good ground cover in cold conservatory

Schefflera arboricola

Dwarf Umbrella Tree ✿

Other names: Dwarf schefflera
Family: Aralia or ivy (*Araliaceae*)
Origin: Taiwan
Appearance: Treelike habit; evergreen; leaves are large, palmate, divided, glossy, on long stalks
Location: All year round, bright to partly shady and airy, in summer also outdoors in a spot sheltered from wind and rain; protect from midday sun; ideally not too warm, in winter cooler, about 54–59°F (12–15°C), variegated-leaved cultivars not below 59°F (15°C); no "cold feet" or cold drafts
Care: Keep evenly but not overly damp, in winter water less if in cool place; avoid waterlogging at all costs; mist often, especially in winter if in warm place; in summer, feed every two to four weeks, in winter, every six weeks; cut back if needed
Use: Handsome ornamental foliage plant for bedrooms and other fairly cool living spaces
Note: The plant contains substances that irritate skin and mucous membranes.

Growth form:
Tree

S

Schefflera elegantissima

False Aralia

Other names: Often still listed under its old name,
Dizygotheca elegantissima
Family: Aralia or ivy (*Araliaceae*)
Origin: New Caledonia
Appearance: Grows treelike; evergreen; leaves are large, finely
pinnate, with toothed margin, dark green to reddish green,
long-stalked
Location: All year round, bright to partly shady and airy,
in summer also outdoors (protected from wind and rain);
no blazing sun; best not too warm, cooler in winter, about
54–59°F (12–15°C); no "cold feet" or cold drafts
Care: Keep evenly but not overly damp, water less in winter
if in cool place; avoid waterlogging at all costs; mist often,
especially in winter if in warm spot; in summer, feed every
two to four weeks, in winter, every six; cut back if needed
Use: Dainty ornament for cooler rooms
Note: The plant contains substances that irritate skin and
mucous membranes.

Growth form:
Climbing shrub

Scindapsus pictus

Satin Pothos

Other names: Pothos vine
Family: Arum lily (*Araceae*)
Origin: Tropical forests of Malaysia
Appearance: Climbing plant, but usually must be trained to climb a pole; leaves are evergreen, almost cordate, leathery, dark green with white spots, in the cultivar 'Argyraeus' the foliage is deep dark green with silvery spots and silvery margin
Location: All year round, bright to partly shady; warm, even in winter not below 64–68°F (18–20°C); no "cold feet"; needs high humidity
Care: Always keep evenly damp, but no waterlogging, don't allow to dry out; mist often; in summer, feed every two weeks, in winter, every four weeks; propagate from stem cuttings at soil and air temperature of about 77°F (25°C)
Use: Elegantly patterned ornamental foliage plant, equally lovely as climber or in hanging planter
Note: The plant contains poisonous substances.

Growth form:
Herbaceous perennial

Selaginella Species

Spikemoss

Family: Spikemoss (*Sellaginellaceae*)
Origin: Widespread in Europe, America, and Africa
Appearance: *S. apoda* and *S. kraussiana* (→ photo) are low, creeping plants with feathery "fronds," *S. martensii* is also carpet-forming but somewhat taller; leaves are small, leathery, scalelike, on branching shoots, which often grow together to form frondlike structures, depending on species, light to medium green, also cultivars with variegated leaves
Location: All year round, partly shady, does not tolerate sun; in summer warm, in winter also cooler at 50°F (10°C); as humid as possible
Care: Keep evenly damp but not wet; drier if overwintered in cool spot, mist often; feed lightly every month; propagate by division or from stem cuttings
Use: For bowls and hanging planters, carpet-forming cultivars good ground cover in conservatory, also good in flower windows, mini-greenhouses, or bottle gardens

Growth form: *Herbaceous perennial*

Soleirolia soleirolii

Baby's Tears

Family: Nettle (*Urticaceae*)
Origin: Wall crevices in Corsica, the Balearics, Sardinia
Appearance: Small, mat-forming herbaceous perennial with thin, sometimes faintly pink stems; leaves are evergreen, tiny, rounded, on short, thin stalks, medium green and glossy, various cultivars with yellow-green, silvery green, or variegated leaves
Location: All year round, bright to partly shady, protect from blazing midday sun; tolerates both room temperature and cooler position; in summer also outdoors, in a sheltered spot
Care: Keep evenly damp, pour water on saucer; in cool position, water less; if in warm place, mist often; in summer, feed every three to four weeks, in winter, every six to eight; propagate by division
Use: For cramped places, in hanging planters, also as fast-growing ground cover in flower windows, mini-greenhouses, or conservatories; also commercially available in bottle gardens

S

Growth form:
Herbaceous perennial
Flowering period:
Summer, fall

Solenostemon scutellarioides

Coleus ✿

Other names: Painted nettle, *Coleus blumei* hybrids
Family: Mint (*Lamiaceae*)
Origin: Cultivars, species from the tropics of Southeast Asia
Appearance: Bushy herbaceous perennials with four-edged stalks; the small coleus has creeping to pendent stems; evergreen; leaves are ovate, notched to toothed, about 3 inches (8 cm) long, commercially available are almost exclusively variegated cultivars with variable yellow, white, green, pink, red, and violet markings; in summer, pale-blue labiate flowers
Location: All year round, bright and sunny; in summer warm, also outdoors, in winter also cooler, at 50°F (10°C)
Care: Water generously in summer, in winter keep drier if in cool place; in summer, feed every two weeks, in winter, every four; cut back hard in spring and also prune repeatedly all year round; propagate from tip cuttings or seed (dark germinator)
Use: Eye-catching house plant, also good in balcony flower box
Note: The plant contains toxins.

Growth form:
Shrub
Flowering period:
June–Aug.

Sparrmannia africana

African Hemp

Family: Linden (*Tiliaceae*)
Origin: Thinly wooded areas in South Africa
Appearance: Shrubby to treelike; in good conditions, white flowers with striking yellow stamens appear; leaves are evergreen, large, rounded to cordate, lobed, soft, hairy, lime green
Location: All year round, very bright and airy, in summer also outdoors; warm in summer, in winter at 50°F (10°C)
Care: Keep evenly and well dampened, in winter water less if in cool position; in summer, feed every one to two weeks, in winter, every three to four; mist often; can easily be cut back; propagate from not overly woody cuttings at about 68°F (20°C)
Use: As solitary specimen in house, also for conservatories, bright hallways and entries, also as container plant
Note: The leaves can cause skin irritations.
Cultivars/Relatives: The cultivar 'Plena' has double flowers.

Growth form: *Climbing shrub*

Tetrastigma voinierianum

Chestnut Vine

Other names: Lizard plant
Family: Grape (*Vitaceae*)
Origin: Forests of Tonkin (Vietnam)
Appearance: Fast-growing climber; tendrils can grow several meters per year; leaves are evergreen, palmate, divided into three to five leaflets, with toothed margins; can grow to 15 inches (40 cm) long; surface dark green and glossy, with brown feltlike hairs beneath
Location: All year round, bright to partly shady, in summer protected from midday sun; warm, but can also be cooler in winter, to 50°F (10°C)
Care: Keep evenly damp in summer, water less in winter if in cool place; in summer, feed weekly, in winter, every three to four weeks; can be cut back hard; needs sturdy trellis; propagate from semilignified cuttings with at least one eye
Use: For large rooms, hallways, conservatories, or as a room divider

Growth form: *Herbaceous perennial*

Tillandsia Species

Air Plants

Family: Bromeliad (*Bromeliaceae*)
Origin: Tropical and subtropical Americas
Appearance: Epiphytic in native habitat, growing on woody plants, cacti, or rocks; roots used only for clinging; water and nutrients absorbed via special scales that give the leaves their gray coloring
Location: Bright to full sun, in summer also outdoors, in winter at 50–59°F (10–15°C)
Care: Glue or tie to pieces of branch or cork, volcanic lava rocks, or clay pipes; from early to late summer mist once to twice daily with lime-poor water, in winter, once to twice weekly; twice a month add very light dose of fertilizer to water
Use: Ideal for epiphyte logs or on decorative surfaces such as gnarled wood, also hanging next to window on suitable surface
Note: The plants contain toxins.

Growth form:
Herbaceous perennial

Tolmiea menziesii

Piggyback Plant ✿

Other names: Youth-on-age
Family: Saxifrage (*Saxifragaceae*)
Origin: Forests on the west coast of North Africa
Appearance: Low herbaceous perennial with creeping or pendulous stems; small plantlets form at base of each leaf; leaves are cordate, slightly lobed, with serrate margins, light to lime green; there are also cultivars with yellow to cream-colored markings
Location: All year round, bright to partly shady, in summer also outdoors if protected from direct sun; airy and not too warm, in winter not below 41°F (5°C)
Care: Water generously in summer, but in winter keep drier if in cool place; in summer, feed every two weeks, in winter only every four to six; propagate from plantlets or from offsets
Use: Undemanding foliage plant with fresh, cheerful effect; also very pretty in hanging planters; ideal for child's room

Growth form:
Herbaceous perennial
Flowering period:
Spring, summer

Tradescantia Species

Spiderwort ✿

Other names: Wandering Jew, chain plant, giant inch plant
Family: Spiderwort (*Commelinaceae*)
Origin: Forests of Central and South America
Appearance: Herbaceous perennials, often rosette-shaped; small white or pink flowers grow in leaf axils; leaves are usually lanceolate to ovate and pointed
Location: All year round, bright and airy, no direct sun; variegated-leaved forms brighter than green-leaved ones; in summer outdoors with protection; warm, in winter cooler, not below 50°F (10°C)
Care: Keep evenly and slightly damp, avoid waterlogging; in winter keep drier if in cool place, water only when soil is dry; in warm place mist often; in summer, feed every two weeks, in winter, only once a month; stems tend to go bare; propagate from tip cuttings in soil or water; easy
Use: Resilient houseplant, suitable also for conservatory, as ground cover, or in hanging planter

Growth form:
Palm

Washingtonia Species

Fan Palm

Other names: Washingtonia, petticoat palm
Family: Palm (*Arecaceae*, *Palmae*)
Origin: Southern California, Arizona, and Mexico
Appearance: Fast-growing, tall palms; deeply cut, large fans with sharply serrate petioles; dead leaves retained on trunk and hang down, forming a "petticoat"; *W. filifera* (→ photo) has gray-green, initially erect, later pendulous leaves with prominent raffia fibers; *W. robusta*: glossy green fans with few or no fibers
Location: All year round, bright to sunny and airy, in summer also outdoors; warm, in winter cool at 46–50°F (8–10°C); does not tolerate radiator heat
Care: Water generously in summer, but avoid waterlogging, keep relatively dry in winter; in summer, feed every two weeks; mist often, especially in winter
Use: Attractive large plant for bright stairwells, entry halls, or cool conservatories

Yucca elephantipes

Spineless Yucca ✿

Family: Agave (*Agavaceae*)
Origin: Dry regions in U.S.A., Mexico
Appearance: Shrubby to treelike; one or more leaf tufts of coarse, sword-shaped leaves
Location: All year round, full sun or at least very bright, in summer outdoors if at all possible; warm, at room temperature, cool in winter at 41–50°F (5–10°C), warmer position also possible
Care: Keep evenly and slightly damp in summer but avoid waterlogging; in winter water occasionally if in cool place; in summer, feeding every three to four weeks suffices; dust leaves occasionally, when repotting choose large planters, as tall and stable as possible, especially for older, very tall plants; even radical cutting back into trunk is tolerated
Use: Popular large plant for ornamental, indoor use, also in cool conservatory; undemanding office plant; young plants also on window ledge
Note: The pointed leaves have sharp edges.

Growth form: *Herbaceous perennial*

Zamioculcas zamiifolia

Aroid Palm ✿

Family: Arum lily (*Araceae*)

Origin: Regions of East and South Africa

Appearance: Stiffly erect; leaves emerge directly from a thick, fleshy rhizome; evergreen; stiff pinnae with petioles thickened and clublike at the base and fleshy midribs, dark green, glossy, individual leaflets often drop off even in young plant, forming small tubers on damp substrate, which take root and become new plants

Location: All year round, bright to partly shady, no direct sun; warm in summer, in winter cooler but not below 60°F (16°C), dislikes "cold feet"

Care: During growing season, keep slightly damp, no water-logging; in winter water less if in cooler place; mist occasionally; in summer, feed every four weeks; propagate by division or from leaf cuttings

Use: Extravagant foliage plant for rooms with proper temperature, or for conservatory

Cacti and Succulents

from A to Z

The sons and daughters of the deserts
and arid regions will truly impress you:
decorative thorns, bizarre growth forms,
and often fantastic flowers make them
amazing potted plants. In addition, most
of them are especially low-maintenance
plants, provided they get enough
sunshine.

Growth form:
Shrub
Flowering period:
Early summer, fall

A

Adenium obesum

Desert Rose

Family: Dogbane (*Apocynaceae*)
Origin: Dry regions of Arabia and East Africa
Flowers: Pinkish red with whitish center, funnel-shaped; often blooming twice, in early summer and in fall, in favorable conditions even throughout the summer
Appearance: Spineless shrub with several stems, erect, with thickened trunk; usually grafted onto an oleander; leaves are broad-ovate, glossy green, leathery, forming clusters at end of stalk
Location: Full sun, warm, in summer also good outdoors, in winter keep at about 59°F (15°C)
Care: Water generously in summer, but let soil dry out between waterings, in winter keep fairly dry, especially in cool location; in summer supply with cactus food every three weeks; propagate from cuttings in spring or from seed
Use: Lavish bloomer for house and conservatory
Note: All parts of the plant contain a poisonous milky sap.

Growth form:
Herbaceous perennial

Agave Species

Agave ❀

Family: Agave (*Agavaceae*)
Origin: Arid regions of the Americas, naturalized in Mediterranean region
Flowers: Pale yellow to light green flowers, in clusters on long stalks; rarely grown indoors; dies after flowering
Appearance: Forms leaf rosettes; leaves are sword-shaped, lanceolate, fleshy, stiff, with sharp spine; *A. americana:* to 6½ feet (2 m) long, gray-green, cultivars with light margins and stripes; *A. filifera* (→ photo): narrow, about 10 inches (25 cm) long, dark green with white fibers; *A. victoriae-reginae:* oblong-triangular, to 11½ inches (30 cm) long, dark green with white markings
Location: All year round, full sun, warm place outdoors in summer, in winter at 50–59°F (10–15°C)
Care: Water sparingly, keep almost dry if overwintered in cool spot; in summer supply cactus food every six weeks
Use: Smaller ones indoors, large ones in conservatory and in container; graphic effect
Note: The sap can cause skin irritations.

Growth form: *Herbaceous perennial*
Flowering period: *Spring, summer*

Aloe Species

Aloe ✿

Family: Aloe (*Aloaceae*)
Origin: Arid regions of South Africa, Madagascar, Cape Verde Islands, Arabia
Appearance: Usually forms leaf rosettes; *A. arborescens* and *A. dichotoma* have many-branched stem topped by rosette; leaves are fleshy, usually lanceolate; *A. arborescen*, bright green, narrow, strongly toothed; *A. aristata* (→ photo, right), dark green with white markings; *A. vera*, gray-green with toothed pink margins; often blooming in cultivation
Location: Full sun, warm; in summer also outdoors, protected from rain; in winter, bright, at 41–50°F (5–10°C)
Care: Needs little water, don't pour water onto rosette, no waterlogging, keep almost dry in winter; in summer feed lightly with cactus food every four to six weeks
Use: For bright, warm rooms
Note: *A. variegata* can irritate the skin; *A. arborescens* and *A. vera* are used as first-aid for burns and skin care.

Growth form:
Globose and columnar cactus
Flowering period:
All year round

Astrophytum Species

Bishop's Cap

Other names: Star cactus
Family: Cactus (*Cactaceae*)
Origin: Desert regions in Mexico and Texas
Flowers: Large, funnel-shaped flowers appear all year round, singly, on the crown; yellow, often with orange-to-red center; throat usually covered with woolly hairs
Appearance: Solitary, variable, bodies usually with few ribs; sea urchin cactus, *A. asterias*, is flat globe, white-spotted and spineless; *A. capricorne*, goat's horn cactus, is rounded to short-columnar and surrounded by long, elastic thorns; the bishop's cap, *A. myriostigma* (→ photo), is globose, spineless, and covered with waxy flecks; *A. ornatum*, the monk's hood, later becomes columnar and has yellow thorns
Location: Sunny and warm, in winter cool, at about 50°F (10°C)
Care: Water sparingly in summer and add cactus food once a month, keep dry in winter
Use: Popular for windowsills, cactus collections

Growth form:
Tree
Flowering period:
Rarely blooms in cultivation

B

Beaucarnea recurvata

Ponytail Palm ✿

Other names: Bottle palm, elephant-foot tree
Family: Dragon tree (*Dracaenaceae*)
Origin: Arid regions of Mexico
Appearance: Treelike, trunk greatly thickened at base, can grow to 6½ feet (2 m) indoors; at the tip are arching, rosette-like leaf tufts; leaves are narrow, to about 3 feet (1 m) long, gray-green
Location: Sunny and warm, in summer also outdoors if protected from rain; in winter, bright and as cool as possible, at about 50°F (10°C)
Care: In summer, keep slightly damp, in winter almost dry if in cool place; tolerates hard water also; in summer, feed lightly every four weeks; propagate from seed or by removal of occasional offsets
Use: For living spaces and conservatory
Note: Newly purchased plants should be introduced to full sun gradually.

Growth form: *Columnar cactus*
Flowering period: *June–Sept.*

Cereus Species

Cereus Cacti ✿

Family: Cactus (*Cactaceae*)
Origin: Arid regions of South America
Flowers: Rare; usually white funnel-shaped flowers in summer, opening only at night; *C. azureus* blooms most often
Appearance: Columnar, deeply ribbed, in old age branching; fast-growing; *C. peruvianus* (night-blooming cereus, → photo): blue-green with red-brown spines; *C. azureus*: blue-frosted with brownish-black spines
Location: Sunny, in summer also outdoors; in winter bright and cool, at about 50°F (10°C)
Care: Water sparingly, *C. peruvianus* only with lime-poor water; keep almost dry in winter; in summer provide with cactus food monthly
Use: Striking cacti for sunny places, provide focal points in cactus collections
Cultivars/Relatives: 'Monstrosus' forms of *C. peruvianus* and *C. azureus* with irregular, bizarre growth are commercially available.

Growth form:
Columnar cactus
Flowering period:
Spring, summer

Cleistocactus Species

Silver Torch Cactus

Family: Cactus (*Cactaceae*)

Origin: Mountainous regions of South America

Flowers: Long, only slightly open, red flowers protrude laterally from body; appearing from spring to summer, depending on column length; *C. baumannii* from 19 inches (50 cm), *C. jujuyensis* from 27 inches (70 cm), *C. smaragdiflorus* from 11½ inches (20 cm), *C. strausii* (→ photo) from 3 feet (1 m)

Appearance: Slender columns, branching at base in some species when full-grown; the numerous ribs are usually thickly covered with spines, *C. strausii* is covered all around with white bristles

Location: Sunny and warm, in summer also outdoors if protected from rain, in winter cooler, at 50–54°F (10–12°C)

Care: In summer, keep slightly damp with lime-poor water, in winter also water occasionally, mist often; don't let column dry out; provide with cactus food every three or four weeks

Use: For sunny windowsill, cactus collection

Growth form:
Shrub
Flowering period:
April–June

Crassula ovata

Jade Plant ❀

Family: Orpine or stonecrop (*Crassulaceae*)
Origin: Arid regions of South Africa
Flowers: Star-shaped single flowers, white to cream-colored, only on older plants; April–June
Appearance: Succulent shrub with thick, heavily branching stems; leaves are succulent, fleshy, usually rounded, glossy green, often red-margined
Location: All year round, very bright to sunny, in summer warm, best outdoors in place protected from rain, cooler in winter, at 50–59°F (10–15°C)
Care: Water sparingly in summer and supply with cactus food every four weeks; in winter water only very little, depending on temperature
Use: Obliging, long-lived, pretty ornamental foliage plant for windowsill and conservatory, larger ones also as container plants
Cultivars/Relatives: *C. arborescens* grows treelike, with gray-green, faintly silvery, red-sprinkled leaves.

Growth form: *Herbaceous perennial*
Flowering period: *Jan.–Oct.*

E

Echeveria Species and Hybrids

Echeveria

Family: Orpine or stonecrop (*Crassulaceae*)
Origin: Arid regions of Mexico, Central and South America
Flowers: White, yellow, pink, orange, red, also multicolored; single flowers usually in pendent, small spikes; depending on species and cultivar, January–October
Appearance: Rosettelike, flowers stalked; leaves are succulent, fleshy, linear, spatulate to broadly triangular, usually with waxy coating; various green shades, pink, red, also multicolored; some covered with thick feltlike hairs
Location: All year round, very bright to sunny, in summer warm, also outdoors in spot protected from rain, cooler in winter, at 41–50°F (5–10°C)
Care: Water sparingly in summer (no water in leaf rosette) and supply with cactus food monthly, in winter keep almost dry
Use: Attractive decoration for very bright places
Cultivars/Relatives: Various cultivars and hybrids (→ photo) are commercially available.

Growth form:
Globose cactus
Flowering period:
Summer

Echinocactus grusonii

Golden Barrel Cactus

Other names: Golden ball cactus, mother-in-law's cushion
Family: Cactus (*Cactaceae*)
Origin: Arid regions of Mexico
Flowers: Silky yellow flowers, appearing only on older plants in summer
Appearance: Globose with many ribs, thickly covered with yellow spines; body often stretches upward in maturity and grows to 4¼ feet (1.3 m) tall and 3 feet (1 m) in diameter
Location: All year round, sunny, warm in summer, also outdoors in protected spot, cooler in winter but not below 50–54°F (10–12°C), otherwise unsightly patches appear
Care: From May to October, keep evenly and slightly damp and provide with cactus food once a month; water seldom in winter; propagate from seed
Use: Pretty for large windowsills, cactus collection, or greenhouse
Cultivars/Relatives: *E. platyacanthus* (giant barrel cactus) has a heavily ribbed body with prominent, stout spines.

Growth form:
Bushy to pendulous
Flowering period:
Spring–summer

E

Epiphyllum Hybrids
Orchid Cactus

Other names: Leaf cactus
Family: Cactus (*Cactaceae*)
Origin: Cultivars, original species from Central/South America
Flowers: Flowers from white through yellow, orange, pink, red to violet and all shades in between, depending on cultivar to 14 inches (35 cm) long; from spring to summer
Appearance: Grows as flat, fleshy, pendulous stems broadened and leaflike, with deeply toothed margins, on which the flowers also appear
Location: Bright all year round, some cultivars also in part shade; in summer best outdoors, in winter cooler, at 50–59°F (10–15°C), some cultivars also at 41°F (5°C)
Care: In summer, keep moderately damp with soft water; supply cactus food every two weeks; mist often; water very sparingly in winter; needs cactus soil containing peat
Use: Attractive ornament for hanging planters or large bowls and pots placed up high
Note: Hybrids are often commercially available (→ photo).

Growth form:
Variable
Flowering period:
All year round

Euphorbia Species

Euphorbia ✿

Other names: Spurge
Family: Spurge (*Euphorbiaceae*)
Origin: Arid regions of Africa and Asia
Flowers: Inconspicuous, surrounded by often brightly colored bracts; flowering period almost all year round
Appearance: Grows globose to shrubby, some with sharp thorns or branching and leggy
Location: Sunny all year round; warm in summer, best outdoors in sheltered spot; cooler in winter, at 50–59°F (10–15°C)
Care: Water sparingly in summer and feed every four weeks; in winter water only rarely if in cool place
Use: Attractive, low-maintenance plants for sunny rooms or conservatory
Note: The milky sap contains substances that may irritate skin and mucous membranes.
Cultivars/Relatives: *E. obesa*, *E. meloformis*, and *E. globosa* are globose; *E. tirucalli* (→ photo), *E. leuconeura*, and *E. grandicornis* grow upward; *E. caput-medusae* has a bizarre appearance.

Growth form:
Shrub
Flowering period:
All year round

E

Euphorbia x lomi

Giant Crown-of-Thorns

Family: Spurge (*Euphorbiaceae*)
Origin: Arid regions of Madagascar
Flowers: Small flowers enclosed by bracts act as real focal point, in the species they are red, in the cultivars also white, yellow, or red; flowering period in winter, some cultivars bloom almost all year round
Appearance: Grows as evergreen, bushy shrub to 3 feet (1 m), with thin, thorny stems; leaves are rich green, obovate, pointed
Location: Sunny all year round; in summer warm, also outdoors in protected spot, cooler in winter, at about 59°F (15°C), otherwise many do not bloom
Care: In summer, water moderately and supply cactus food every four weeks, in winter water very sparingly, can be cut back after bloom
Use: Undemanding ornamental plant for indoors, cultivars with long stems can also be trimmed into shape
Note: The milky sap can irritate the skin.

Graptopetalum bellum

Chihuahua Flower

Other names: Tacitus
Family: Orpine or stonecrop (*Crassulaceae*)
Origin: Arid regions of Central America
Flowers: Pink to crimson, five-petaled; February–May
Appearance: Flat to semiglobose, tall rosette of gray-green, fleshy, pointed leaves arranged like roof tiles
Location: Very bright, also sunny, but protected from blazing midday sun; warm, but cool in winter at 50–59°F (10–15°C) or no flower production
Care: Water moderately, keep somewhat damp while flowering but almost dry in winter; until August feed every three to four weeks; propagate from leaf cuttings
Use: Charming small succulent, also attractive when not blooming; for bright windowsills
Note: All parts of the plant are poisonous and can irritate the skin.
Cultivars/Relatives: *G. paraguayense* (ghost plant) has leaves that change color.

Growth form:
Globose cactus
Flowering period:
Spring–fall

G

Gymnocalycium Species

Chin Cactus

Family: Cactus (*Cactaceae*)
Origin: Arid regions of South America
Flowers: Flowers grow to 2 inches (5 cm) across, often appearing even on young plants; the species differ in their flower colors: *G. andreae*, yellow, *G. baldianum* (→ photo), dark red, *G. denudatum*, white, *G. gibbosum*, white, *G. multiflorum*, pink-white; spring–fall
Appearance: Flattened to rounded globe with notched, bumpy ribs and dark spines; the plaid cactus (*G. mihanovichii* var. *friedrichii*) is always grown on graft, as it has no chlorophyll and cannot survive on its own
Location: Bright all year round but no full sun, warm in summer, also outdoors if protected from rain, in winter at about 50°F (10°C), plaid cactus not below 59°F (15°C)
Care: In summer, water moderately and provide cactus food every four weeks, in winter keep almost dry
Use: Pretty cacti for windowsills

Growth form: *Herbaceous perennial*

Haworthia Species

Haworthia ✿

Other names: Star plant
Family: Aloe (*Aloaceae*)
Origin: Arid regions of South Africa
Appearance: Tall, succulent rosette plants, growing to about 8 inches (20 cm), usually stemless or only short-stemmed; leaves are linear to broad-ovate or triangular, fleshy, succulent, often with small bumps or warts, and with toothed or fringed margins
Location: All year round, bright but no blazing midday sun; in summer, warm, also outdoors in protected spot, cooler in winter, at 50–59°F (10–15°C), a bit warmer if necessary
Care: In summer, water sparingly, provide with cactus food every four weeks, in winter dampen only occasionally; propagate from offsets or seed
Use: Graphic effect for bright rooms
Cultivars/Relatives: Popular are *H. attenuata* (→ photo) and *H. fasciata* (zebra plant), in which the white tubercles beneath the leaves merge to form cross-bands.

Growth form:
Bushy to treelike
Flowering period:
May–June

J

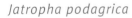

Jatropha podagrica

Buddha Belly Plant

Family: Spurge (*Euphorbiaceae*)
Origin: Arid regions of Central America and West Indies
Flowers: Small, coral-red flowers borne in dense inflores-cences on long stalks, May–June
Appearance: Grows as branchy, fleshy, deciduous succulent with thickened, bottle-shaped trunk; branches covered with thorny stipules; about 24 inches (60 cm) tall; leaves are large, rough, three- to five-lobed, dark green on top, with whitish coating beneath
Location: All year round, bright to sunny, warm in summer, cooler in winter, at 50–59°F (10–15°C)
Care: Water moderately during bloom, otherwise keep drier, especially after leaves drop in fall; in summer, supply with cactus food once a month
Use: With its bizarre form, an unusual, but low-maintenance plant for bright rooms
Note: All parts of the plant are poisonous.

Growth form: *Herbaceous perennial*
Flowering period: *July–Nov.*

Lithops Species

Living Stones

Other names: Flowering stones
Family: Fig-marigold or ice plant (*Aizoaceae*)
Origin: Arid regions of South Africa
Flowers: White or yellow, daisylike; July–November
Appearance: Fleshy, upside-down cone-shaped leaf pairs growing deep in the ground, fused except for small fissure, blunt surfaces are structured, patterned or transparent; usually crowded in dense clumps
Location: Full sun all year round; warm, in summer also outdoors if protected from rain; in winter at 54–59°F (12–15°C)
Care: Water very sparingly, as of September keep completely dry until old leaves are dried up; no feeding required; must be potted in very good, permeable cactus substrate
Use: Fascinating plants for south-facing windows, particularly for succulent collections
Cultivars/Relatives: *Fenestraria* (baby toes) is similar.

Growth form:
Globose cactus
Flowering period:
All year round

M

Mammillaria Species

Pincushion Cactus

Family: Cactus (*Cactaceae*)
Origin: Arid regions of U.S.A., Mexico, South America
Flowers: Appearing all year round, usually in a wreath around the globose body; color ranges from white through yellow, orange, pink, and red to purple (*M. zeilmanniana*, → photo); berrylike, often bright-red fruit develops
Appearance: Usually growing as small, often colony-forming globe cacti, whose bodies have no ribs, however, but are covered all around with tubercles; generally thickly covered with spines, sometimes also with decorative hairs
Location: Full sun, protect green species, which have few spines, from blazing midday sun; in summer warm, also outdoors with rain protection, cooler in winter, at 46–54°F (8–12°C), green forms around 59°F (15°C)
Care: In summer, water sparingly with lime-poor water and supply with cactus food every four weeks, keep dry in winter; propagate from seed or offsets
Use: For sunny windowsills, cactus collection

Growth form: *Jointed cactus*
Flowering period: *July–Sept.*

Opuntia Species

Prickly Pear Cactus

Family: Cactus (*Cactaceae*)
Origin: Arid regions of North and South America
Flowers: Yellow, pink, red; July–September
Appearance: Depending on species, quite variable; flattened, disk-shaped limbs with dot-like groups of tiny spines in *O. microdasys* (bunny ears); cylindrical limbs with very coarse spines in *O. bigelovii* (teddy-bear cholla)
Location: Very bright, best in full sun; warm, in summer also outdoors, in winter at 50°F (10°C)
Care: Water sparingly, keep almost dry in winter; until August supply with cactus food every three to four weeks; propagate by removal of offsets
Use: Charming to bizarre shapes for south-facing windows, cactus collections, small desert gardens
Note: Opuntias have tiny spines equipped with barbed hooks that dig painfully into the skin and are hard to remove.

Growth form:
Shrub
Flowering period:
Spring

P

Pachypodium Species

Madagascar Palm

Family: Dogbane (*Apocynaceae*)
Origin: Arid regions of Madagascar
Flowers: White, in umbels; only on older plants; spring
Appearance: Growing with thickened, columnar trunk and palmlike leaf tuft
Location: Sunny to bright and warm, best on windowsill above a radiator, in winter not below 64°F (18°C)
Care: Water generously in summer, but avoid waterlogging; in winter water only sparingly (or leaves will drop), but never allow to dry out; in spring and summer, supply with cactus food at monthly intervals
Use: Lends desert flair to warm rooms, larger plants can be used as sculptures to serve as focal point
Note: All the parts contain a poisonous milky sap; the leaf spines can cause injury.
Cultivars/Relatives: *P. geyai* is known for its narrow, faintly silvery leaf tufts, *P. lamerei* (→ photo) has broader, fresh dark-green leaves.

Growth form:
Globose cactus
Flowering period:
Spring

Rebutia Species

Crown Cactus

Other names: Rebutia
Family: Cactus (*Cactaceae*)
Origin: Mountains in Argentina and Bolivia
Flowers: Funnel-shaped to broad star-shaped flowers in brilliant red, orange, yellow, or white, always borne in a crown surrounding the body; spring
Appearance: Globose with spirally arranged tubercles, colony-forming, with thin, bristlelike spines
Location: Sunny to bright, no blazing sun; ideal is a place warm by day, very cool at night; in winter at 41°F (5°C)
Care: Water very sparingly, feed every three to four weeks; keep almost dry in winter; propagate from offsets or seed (light germinator)
Use: South-facing windows in cool rooms; in collections
Cultivars/Relatives: There are many species of this freely flowering, easy-care cactus, often sold under the generic name *Rebutia*. *R. albiflora* has white flowers, *R. krainziana* has red-yellow.

Growth form:
Jointed cactus
Flowering period:
March– May

R

Rhipsalidopsis Species and Hybrids

Easter Cactus

Other names: Often still commercially available as *Hatiora*
Family: Cactus (*Cactaceae*)
Origin: Tropical mountain forests of Brazil
Flowers: In early spring fuchsia-like flowers borne at stem ends, depending on species and cultivars, in red or pink
Appearance: Epiphytic habit; slightly drooping stems made up of flattened, smooth, often red-margined joints
Location: Bright to partly shady, no blazing sun; warm, cooler in winter
Care: Keep moderately damp with lime-free water, supply with cactus food every two to three weeks; put in cool place as of February to promote flower production
Use: Magnificent ornamental flowering plant for warm rooms, also for hanging planters
Cultivars/Relatives: *R. gaertneri*, with red flowers, considered true Easter cactus; cultivars of *R.* x *graeseri* (→ photo) differ only in flower color; reddish pink flowers give *R. rosea* name of rose Easter cactus.

Growth form:
Twig-like cactus
Flowering period:
Winter

Rhipsalis Species

Rhipsalis Cactus

Other names: Coral cactus
Family: Cactus (*Cactaceae*)
Origin: Tropical forests of South America
Flowers: In winter, star-shaped flowers in white or light yellow, in some cases fragrant
Appearance: Long, very thin, pendulous joints resembling bulrushes or twigs
Location: Bright, but not in full sun, warm and humid; cooler in winter, at 50–59°F (10–15°C)
Care: Water amply with lime-free water, mist often; feed lightly every two weeks to promote flowering; in fall, keep drier for two months
Use: Unusual plant for hanging planters in warm rooms, also especially lovely atop columns
Cultivars/Relatives: *R. baccifera* has light green stems; *R. cereuscula*, dark green and light green; *R. clavata*, medium green, thicker toward ends; *R. paradoxa*, squared stems. In *R. pachyptera* the dark-green stems seem like broad leaves.

Growth form: *Jointed cactus*
Flowering period: *Nov.–March*

S

Schlumbergera Species and Hybrids

Christmas Cactus

Other names: Claw cactus
Family: Cactus (*Cactaceae*)
Origin: Tropical forests of Brazil
Flowers: In late December, numerous, orchid-like flowers open, with color depending on species and cultivar, from white through pink and red to violet
Appearance: Epiphytic habit with leaf-like joints, which are notched or toothed and bear no spines
Location: All year round, bright to partly shady and warm, in summer also outdoors, cooler in winter, at 54–59°F (12–15°C); sensitive to change of location
Care: As of September, keep cool and dry, as of December put in warmer spot and keep moderately damp, using only decalcified water, mist occasionally
Use: For warm rooms, during dormancy in cool rooms
Cultivars/Relatives: *S. truncata* is the true Christmas cactus. The *S.* hybrids (→ photo) are similar; the flower color depends on cultivar.

Growth form:
Herbaceous perennial
Flowering period:
Summer

Sedum Species

Sedum ✿

Other names: Stonecrop
Family: Orpine or stonecrop (*Crassulaceae*)
Origin: Arid regions of Central America and Japan
Flowers: In summer, white to light pink star-shaped flowers in umbrella-like inflorescences
Appearance: Initially grows erect to creeping, later has pendulous stems; leaves are small and fleshy, gray-green to reddish, crowded together along stem axis
Location: Ideally, sunny all year round, at least very bright; moderately warm, in winter cool, at 41–50°F (5–10°C); in summer also outdoors (protected from rain)
Care: Water very sparingly; in spring and summer months, supply with cactus food every four weeks
Use: For hanging planters in sunny, south-facing windows, effective on pedestals or columns
Cultivars/Relatives: *S. morganianum* (burro tail) has tail-like hanging stems; 'Baby Burro Tail' stays daintier; *S.* x *rubrotinctum* (Christmas cheer → photo) is similar.

Growth form:
Herbaceous perennial
Flowering period:
Summer

S

Senecio Species and Hybrids

Ragwort, Groundsel ❀

Other names: Old-man-in-the-spring, string of pearls
Family: Aster / daisy / sunflower (*Asteraceae*)
Origin: Arid regions of Africa, Peninsular India, Mexico
Flowers: White to pink composite flowers in summer (only on older plants)
Appearance: Produces thin, long, pendent, only slightly branched stems; leaves are rounded, thickened, pointed, arranged on the stems like pearls on a string
Location: Sunny to partly shady, in summer also outdoors, in winter best at 50–54°F (10–12°C)
Care: Water sparingly, in spring and summer supply with cactus food every two weeks
Use: Low-maintenance plant for hanging planters and columns; for house and conservatory
Note: All parts of the plant contain toxins.
Cultivars/Relatives: In *S. herreianus* (→ photo), the globe-shaped leaves have fine lines; *S. rowleyanus* has translucent stripes; *S. citriformis* has light-green leaves.

Designing with Plants

Attractive plants are available in a wide range of choices. You can find vibrant foliage plants and brilliantly colored flowering plants that will harmonize with the style of your home and create a comfortable, cozy atmosphere and an increased sense of well-being.

Make Designing Fun

Integrating plants into your surroundings in a harmonious way is an art that's not hard to master. If you follow a few ground rules, you'll be sure to get the style right.

Colors and Shapes—An Embarrassment of Riches

Elegant monotones, subtle tone-on-tone, or a bright pop of color—houseplants offer a broad palette of colors to use for very different effects. In addition, the shapes of leaves and branches and the overall look give you a host of possibilities for making your surroundings comfortable and livable.

From your very first glance, the selection available in your local garden center tells you that green plants don't simply come in green. Each green is different from the next. Delicate light green has a light, springlike effect, whereas strong dark green makes a more severe, elegant impression. The leaf surfaces—smooth, wrinkled, furrowed, waxy, hairy—go one step further to make green dazzling in all shades. Quite a number of plants present silvery gray, blue-green, variegated, or patterned leaves that can hold their own against colorful flowers. Besides leaf colors, flowers as well as fruits enliven the plants' fashion show with their brilliant hues. Light, dainty shades create a romantic, cheerful look, while dark, intense colors often push themselves to the fore.

Always choose colors that go with your furnishings; match the plants to the

Pendulous stems are most effective when the plant is on a table or pedestal.

Different colors can create different effects:

➤ Red: invigorating, powerful, fiery, stimulating, warm
➤ Yellow: festive, cheerful, brightening, warm, exhilarating
➤ Blue: fresh, calming, cool, relaxing
➤ Violet: soothing, gentle, cool if they lean toward blue-violet
➤ Pink: gentle, friendly, brightening, playful, peaceful
➤ White: light, brightening, calming, neutral, cool, fresh
➤ Green: soothing, balancing, natural, gentle, friendly

furniture, rugs, and window treatments. Create exciting contrasts, for example, by combining plants that have bright red flowers with dark furniture. For an understated look, choose pastel colors, which fit into almost every living environment. You can also use diverse growth forms to achieve different effects.

Plants that grow upward with little branching have an austerely elegant look, while spreading, bushy ones seem casual and cozy. Rosette plants delight with their precise symmetry, and hanging and climbing plants weave filmy garlands. Use growth forms and colors to achieve special effects with your plants.

Solo or in a Group

Always think of houseplants as sculptures too, deserving to be presented as art objects in your room. When buying plants, consider whether they require a starring role or can fit easily into their surroundings.

➤ **Expressive soloists:** The more majestic, picturesque, gorgeous, or bizarre a house plant looks, the more it deserves to have a spot all to itself. Alone, a palm, large fern, showy medinilla, or bottle tree need not compete with any other plant and automatically is a focal point. However, not all solo artists are decidedly stately in size; a small, carefully chosen plant can definitely be the star of the room. Plants with these characteristics are the best choices for use as solitary specimens: large leaves, such as philodendron; foliage that has lively markings and colors, like caladium; strikingly large flowers, like hibiscus, or numerous flowers, like azalea; unusual growth forms, like bottle tree, standards, plants with intertwining trunks, and artfully trained climbers.

➤ **Group harmony:** You can put several plants of one cultivar as well as entirely different species together in a group. Always make sure that all the group's members have the same location requirements. Combinations of plants of one species—three moth orchids or five peperomias, for example—are extremely charming. More excitement is created when you combine various cultivars of a single species, such as African violets with different-colored blooms. Plants that exhibit at least one common characteristic, such as coloring or a specific growth habit, can be united in a playful way. Plants with the same form can be grouped in any number you choose, even as pairs. High contrast is

Such a pretty fern deserves to have a one-man show.

> **The graphic growth forms blend well with the subtle earth tones.**

provided by plant groups whose members differ in growth form, foliage, and flower color: for example, an upright dracaena, a lacy asparagus fern, and an African violet. Make sure always to have an uneven number of plants in arrangements of this kind.

EXTRA TIP

Impressive Soloists
➤ African hemp (*Sparrmannia africana*)
➤ Dracaena (*Dracaena* species)
➤ Dumb cane (*Dieffenbachia*)
➤ Fiddle-leaf fig (*Ficus lyrata*)
➤ Palms, such as the Kentia palm (*Howea*)
➤ Spineless yucca (*Yucca elephantipes*)
➤ Split-leaf philodendron (*Monstera deliciosa*)
➤ Weeping fig (*Ficus benjamina*)

Designing with Plants

1 Hanging plants with a difference

2 Prettily adorned

3 Kalanchoe, elegantly wrapped

4 An Asian look

Bold colors **5**

Pretty in Pots

Every houseplant, whether simple or majestic, benefits from a packaging that harmonizes with its distinctive quality, that is, from an appropriate decorative container. Even purists who want the focus always on the plant, with nothing distracting from its natural beauty, can't dispense with a planter: one that's as unobtrusive as possible, of course. The opposite extreme is a showy, attention-grabbing container in which the plant plays second fiddle, always overshadowed.

First and foremost, a planter must be tailored to the plant's needs. It has to provide adequate room for the roots and the surrounding substrate. Plants can go straight into handsome flowerpots of clay, ceramics, or plastic, provided they have water drainage holes. Usually, however, indoor plants are in pots that are fairly unattractive, though practical. Placing flowerpots in cachepots instantly gives plants extra charm. Garden centers offer innumerable versions of them, made of different materials, in diverse shapes, and in a wide array of colors.

A cachepot should underscore the distinctive quality of a plant and bring its elegance to the fore. In addition, planters establish a visual connection between the plants and the room. If you choose identical or at least similar planters for a room, the arrangement is bound to succeed.

EXTRA TIP

Decorative Accessories

Think about adding a few decorative touches to make your houseplants look their best. Decorative plant markers can provide spots of color when your plants are not in bloom. Little figures hung on the edge of the pot can make even simple green plants into real eyecatchers. Decorative climbing frames and plant stakes are pretty and practical at the same time.

Gorgeous Plants All Over the House

> **Different shades of green and distinct shapes have a calming effect.**

Depending on its use, every living space offers a microclimate of its own for your plants, and you should keep this in mind when making your choices.

Living Spaces

As a rule, living rooms are the biggest, brightest, and warmest rooms. These spaces, where the greatest part of daily life takes place, are precisely where many people want really sumptuous ornamental plants. They are spots where you can thoroughly enjoy calming greens and cheerful flower colors. From the wide range available in garden centers, you should select plants that are an attractive complement to your furnishings and also will thrive in the light and temperature conditions your home offers.

Large window surfaces and balcony and patio doors admit a great deal of light, which plants welcome enthusiastically. Even next to south-facing windows, where heat can build up in summer, you can place yucca, candelabra-like

Beautiful plants create a pleasant working atmosphere.

euphorbias, or palms as "sentinels" or "live room dividers." If you want to grow less sun-loving species there, provide some shade at midday. Because they are usually heated all year round, living spaces usually are best suited for many plants native to tropical regions. Plants with gorgeous flowers, such as showy medinilla and orchids, add bold accents, while lush green plants like philodendrons create a pleasant home environment.

The usually generous dimensions of the room often make it possible to accommodate large plants as green, living sculptures. Solitary plants such as palms, weeping fig, split-leaf philodendron, and zedoary root can be placed right next to windows. The farther you move them from the windows, the sooner you'll have to consider additional lighting (→ page 9).

During the winter months, tropical plants in particular feel that they're in good hands because of the heated

(→ page 9)

EXTRA TIP

Green in Your Study and Office

With lots of green foliage and colorful flowers, you can create a pleasant working atmosphere that benefits more than just your psyche. Dry air is made more humid by plants, and dust and pollutants are filtered out by leaves. For your "office flora," choose robust species with ample foliage, ideally grown hydroponically or in granulated clay, such as rubber tree plant, cast iron plant, split-leaf philodendron, Swedish ivy, queen's tears, dracaena, centipede tongavine, peace lily, ivy, Chinese evergreen, and spider plant.

air, but they are quick to suffer from overly dry air. Position air humidifiers in the room.

> **Waking up is a different experience altogether when you're greeted by such a sight.**

Bedrooms

Waking up in the morning and being greeted by the refreshing sight of plants—relaxing in the evening and being guided into slumber by plants that are perfect dreams: that's what paradise must be like. Make this wish come true by equipping your bedroom with beautiful growing things.

Today bedrooms are far more than mere places to get a night's rest. They are retreats, places to relax, read a book, and recoup your energy. At such times, plants are very welcome as feasts for the eyes and pick-me-ups. To really show off your green favorites, position them sparingly—less is often more in this context.

And this way, every plant can display its assets to good advantage. You can calmly rebut the stubborn preconception that at night, plants rob humans of the oxygen they need and therefore have no place in a bedroom. Just the opposite is true. Plants improve the air in a room. Health problems can arise in a very different way: Mold may grow on potting soil that is constantly damp. Even if you are allergic to mold, however, you need not dispense with ornamental plants. Grow your plants hydroponically; mold almost never develops with this method.

Since bedrooms frequently face east or north, they generally have dim light. Gentle morning sunshine or nothing but indirect sunlight often do not make the room bright enough for sun-loving plants, but species that enjoy partial or even full shade are especially content here. At the same time, lower temperatures predominate in bedrooms, or warm days may alternate with cooler nights. That makes the air more humid, which many plants greatly appreciate. The nighttime drop in temperature, too,

is something many plants find beneficial. Gardenia and jasmine, for example, also appreciate the softly lit, cool, humid environment. They bloom very profusely in such surroundings and develop an especially intense scent. If this causes headaches, you can simply replace these scented plants with unscented ones that have equally lovely flowers, such as cyclamen and Cape primrose.

EXTRA TIP

Recommended Plants
➤ Azalea
(*Rhododendron* hybrids)
➤ Bush ivy
(x *Fatshedera lizei*)
➤ Camellia
(*Camellia* hybrids)
➤ Cyclamen
(*Cyclamen persicum*)
➤ Hydrangea
(*Hydrangea* hybrids)
➤ Japanese aralia
(*Fatsia japonica*)
➤ Sago palm
(*Cycas revolute*)

Children's Rooms

Children have a special liking for plants, particularly if they have colorful flowers, bear tempting little fruits, or develop into unusual shapes. With playful curiosity, children want to learn everything about their green roommates. This may mean that leaves are plucked off and carefully scrutinized, pretty flowers are picked for Mom, a flowerpot is accidentally overturned, or a plant is overeagerly watered.

Plants should be able to uncomplainingly accept all these little rash behaviors in a child's room. For these reasons, your motto should be: Keep it simple, robust,

EXTRA TIP

Hazard-Free Flowers
In general, choose only nonpoisonous plants. Also avoid species that contain skin irritants or can trigger allergic reactions. Pay close attention to the notes and the corresponding symbols in the plant profiles. Plants that can cause injury, such as Madagascar palm, agaves, or prickly pear cactus, have no place in a child's room.

Umbrella plants and ragwort are also appropriate for children's rooms.

PLANTS THAT CHILDREN ENJOY

➤ African violet
(*Saintpaulia ionantha*)
➤ Air plant
(*Bryophyllum pinnatum*)
➤ Jade plant
(*Crassula ovata*)
➤ Kalanchoe
(*Kalanchoe blossfeldiana*)
➤ Piggyback plant
(*Tolmiea menziesii*)

➤ Polka-dot plant
(*Hypoestes phyllostachya*)
➤ Prairie gentian
(*Eustoma grandiflorum*)
➤ Queen's tears
(*Billbergia nutans*)
➤ String of pearls
(*Senecio rowleyanus*)
➤ Umbrella plant
(*Cyperus* species)

and low-maintenance, and remember that "children's plants" also should look as cute or as fantastic and bizarre as possible. Then they will be fun for the children.

In addition, children need your guidance: Take your offspring with you when you choose the plants, explain their needs, and—most importantly—demonstrate how to take care of them. That is how children learn to understand plants, accept the responsibility for them, and give them the proper care. These experiences will make a life-long impression on them, and their green thumbs will be pre-programmed.

So that the little people in your household can easily see the plants, you should put them at eye level—

The brilliantly colored Gerbera daisy can have a positive effect on your mood.

ideally in unbreakable plastic planters. Where no surface is available, you can use hanging planters.

241

Kitchen and Bathrooms

The kitchen is considered the coziest and most convivial room in every home—although its furnishings are primarily practical. But family members and guests get together here and look forward to a pleasant meal. Visual pleasure should be no less important, so kitchen plants are called for.

Bathrooms are also primarily functional rooms. Tiles, mirror, and fixtures with smooth surfaces contribute to good hygiene but offer little in the way of charm. Even a few leafy vines and flowers can transform the stiff, cold look of the bathroom into a snug environment.

Umbrella plants can easily tolerate the high humidity of a bathroom.

A pretty dab of color—ideal for the kitchen.

➤ **Plants for small kitchens:** The smaller a kitchen is, the faster conditions in the room can change, especially when the room is fully enclosed. It may have been warm while cooking was going on or humid when the dishes were being washed, but outside "business hours" it often can be cold and dry. In addition, the air is burdened with oily cooking fumes. Robust, undemanding plants such as spider plant, centipede tongavine, snake plant, or small coconut palms tolerate these conditions and thus are uncomplaining kitchen dwellers—provided they are carefully tended and their leaves are regularly freed of the oily, dirty film that builds up.

➤ **Plants for big kitchens:** Spacious eat-in kitchens or kitchens that are open to living areas give you more latitude in choosing plants. Basically you can view any warmth-loving species as a candidate, provided the lighting conditions are right and the location is not directly next to the stove. Put plants on etageres, consoles, or wall shelves to keep them out of your way.

➤ **Plants for bathrooms:** A tropical climate, warm and steamy—such ideal conditions exist in bathrooms, at least temporarily. Warmth and humidity are usually adequate, but often the absence of large window surfaces means that there is not enough light. Shade plants can play leading roles here: ferns, prayer plant, or begonias. Flamingo flower, bromeliads, and orchids supply an exotic air. Baby's tears, gynura, and fittonia make even cramped bathrooms into real spas. Take advantage of the mirror's effect: Plants placed directly in front of it seem twice as luxuriant.

Hallway and Stairwell

In the entry area of your apartment or house, you welcome visitors, but you also want to be greeted with equal enthusiasm. Plants can make the reception very pleasant and invite guests to stay a while. In choosing species, remember that entries and stairwells generally are cool and subject to drafts. Generously proportioned front halls and spacious stairwells that are flooded with light function almost as conservatories and can certainly tolerate wide-spreading plants such as *Ficus* species, yucca, split-leaf philodendron, Norfolk Island pine, lady palm, Hesper palm, bush ivy trained to grow up a peat stake, or a rambling evergreen grape. Slender, stiffly upright species like cast iron plant and snake plant make themselves small here and are unlikely to get in the way.

If your available space is not quite so generous, and if your front hallway is dark as well, then plants that stay small and are more shade-tolerant have their turn at a starring role. Ivy, creeping fig, hart's tongue fern, strawberry begonia, rosary vine, maidenhair vine, and true myrtle will nestle into small corners and bubble over with charm nonetheless. If you don't want unrelieved green, simply add a few uncomplicated flowering plants, such as *Begonia elatior* hybrids and hydrangeas, or seasonal plants like primroses, bellflowers, impatiens, or fall chrysanthemums.

This weeping fig offers a hearty welcome.

PRETTY SEASONAL DECORATIONS

NAME	FLOWERING PERIOD, FLOWER COLOR	LOCATION, NOTES
Autumn crocus *Colchicum* species and hybrids	Aug.–Oct.; pink, violet, white	Sunny, moderately warm; all parts are poisonous
Chrysanthemum *Chrysanthemum* species and hybrids	Aug.–Dec.; many colors	Bright, cool
Crocus *Crocus* species and hybrids	Feb.; yellow, white, pink, purple, violet	Bright, cool; poisonous
Daffodil *Narcissus* species and hybrids	March–May; yellow, orange, white	Partly shady, cool; all parts are poisonous
Gerbera daisy *Gerbera* species and hybrids	April–Oct., also all year round; many colors	Bright, moderately warm, cool in winter
Hyacinth *Hyacinthus orientalis*	Dec.–May; many colors, strongly scented	Bright, cool
Iron Cross plant *Oxalis deppei*	Winter; Pink	Sunny to bright, quite cool; all parts are poisonous
Tulip *Tulipa* species and hybrids	April–May; many colors, also multicolored	Sunny to partly shady, cool; all parts are poisonous

ALREADY DESCRIBED IN PROFILE SECTION

Designing with Plants

PLANTS FOR BRIGHT AND SUNNY PLACES

Air plants	Page 194	Jade plant	Page 208
Allamanda	Page 29	Jerusalem cherry plant	Page 93
Baby bamboo	Page 174	Kalanchoe	Page 69
Begonia elatior hybrids	Page 34	Kangaroo paw	Page 31
Bellflower	Page 41	Livistona	Page 155
Buddha belly plant	Page 217	Madagascar palm	Page 221
Bush violet	Page 36	Ornamental pepper	Page 42
Chihuahua flower	Page 214	Pink quill	Page 97
Coconut palm	Page 129	Poor man's orchid	Page 90
Coleus	Page 191	Ragwort, groundsel	Page 227
Crown cactus	Page 222	Sedum	Page 226
Cymbidium orchids	Page 52	Swedish ivy	Page 173
Echeveria	Page 209	True myrtle	Page 160
Fan palm	Page 197	Umbrella plant	Page 136
Hesper palm	Page 116		

PLANTS FOR SUNNY PLACES

African blood lily	Page 60	Flame lily	Page 58
Agave	Page 202	Giant crown-of-thorns	Page 213
Aloe	Page 203	Golden barrel cactus	Page 210
Bishop's cap	Page 204	Living stones	Page 218
Bottle tree	Page 115	Pincushion cactus	Page 219
Cereus cacti	Page 206	Ponytail palm	Page 205
Chilean jasmine	Page 71	Prickly pear cactus	Page 220
Date palm	Page 168	Rosary vine	Page 122
Desert rose	Page 201	Rose	Page 88
Egyptian star cluster	Page 83	Silver torch cactus	Page 207
Eugenia species	Page 141	Spineless yucca	Page 198
Euphorbia	Page 212	Winter jasmine	Page 67

All the other species described in the profile section like bright locations, with the exceptions of fittonia, maidenhair fern, elephant ear, and spikemoss.

PLANTS FOR SHADY PLACES

Fittonia	Page 147	Japanese aralia	Page 143
Ivy	Page 149	Maidenhair fern	Page 103

PLANTS FOR PARTLY SHADY PLACES

Index of Plants

Page numbers in **bold** refer to photos.

Appendix

Photo Credits, Copyright